# ARE YOU RANGERS IN DISGUISE?

## THE UPS, DOWNS – AND UPS OF REPORTING ON QPR

# ARE YOU
## RANGERS IN
## DISGUISE?

### THE UPS, DOWNS – AND UPS
### OF REPORTING ON QPR

## BEN KOSKY
### FOREWORD BY KEVIN GALLEN

DB PUBLISHING

First Published in Great Britain in 2020 by DB Publishing,
an imprint of JMD Media Ltd

ISBN 9781780916088

# CONTENTS

# FOREWORD
## by Kevin Gallen

Anyone who knows me, knows just how big a part of my life QPR has always been. I was fortunate enough to spend most of my playing career in a Rangers shirt, but I was a fan long before then and ever since I kicked my last ball for the club.

We lived in East Acton, about 15 or 20 minutes' walk from the ground, and my dad was – and still is – a season ticket holder. It was an amazing time to be a QPR fan when I started going regularly in the 1982-83 season – we had a really good team, a world-class manager in Terry Venables and we got promoted, then did really well the next year in the First Division.

My brothers, Joe and Steve, were training at Watford, so I went there as well, playing right-back at that time. I was happy at Watford but, when I was nearly 14, QPR said they wanted to sign me on schoolboy forms. How could I turn that down? QPR were my team, after all.

It was like a dream for me – I'd been watching players like Paul Parker, Alan McDonald and Roy Wegerle and it wasn't too long before I was training with them too. For me there was no lack of motivation. I'd be saying 'I want to get in this team and play with my heroes'.

QPR felt like a real family club at that time and I loved being around the place. You knew everyone on the backroom staff, people like Sheila Marson and Terry Springett and, on the playing side, there were so many other lads who'd come through from the youth team as I'd done. We had a squad full of players who were hungry to do well for themselves and hungry to do well for the team.

Ian Holloway was one of those and he brought back that same kind of team spirit when he was manager. He got players in who were good characters too – Birchy, Paul Furlong and Gareth Ainsworth for instance, people who would run through a brick wall for the team. The senior players would run the dressing-room for Ollie in the same way Ray Wilkins had done under Gerry Francis and it really felt like QPR were on the way back.

And then... it all went crackers. The fabric of the club changed and you didn't know who was coming or going. Before long you had managers getting sacked and new players arriving all the time – it felt like playing a game of Championship Manager, only for real.

Of course, after I'd left QPR, I still followed what was going on and I didn't like to see how the people in charge were trying to become 'the Chelsea of the Championship', showing off about all the money they'd got and the celebrities who had started turning up. Fans of other teams who used to have a soft spot for QPR were now saying 'your club's a shambles' and it's easy to get angry and take that to heart.

To be honest, for 99.9 per cent of fans, all they care about is getting three points and being entertained, which is totally understandable. Very few fans are that bothered about what's going on behind the scenes. But when you're a player and you've been in behind the scenes, you take a different perspective – and it's probably similar for a journalist like Ben, as a QPR fan reporting on the club. It's difficult when you know more of the ins and outs and you can end up getting stick from other fans because of that. We might have different opinions but, in the end, we all care about the club.

It's always great to bump into QPR fans and I still love coming to Loftus Road with my son, who loves it too. Hopefully, we'll be back there supporting the team just as soon as fans are allowed in again.

Come on you R's!

# ACKNOWLEDGEMENTS

'Have you ever thought about writing a book?' It's a question I've been asked many times, sometimes by professional colleagues, more often by friends who were probably bored senseless when I started whingeing about whether my career was actually going anywhere. But finally, after years of agreeing that writing a book might be a good idea but failing to put it into practice, here it is! Not the longest book ever written, I admit, but that makes it less of a squeeze to fit it onto the shelf, and putting this book together has been an enjoyable and fulfilling experience for me. I hope you'll get something out of reading it, too – whether you're a QPR supporter, a fan of football in general, or maybe someone who takes a passing interest in sports journalism. If not... well, by way of upgrading the old-school phrase 'I'll see you outside' to the 21st century, feel free to look me up on Twitter (@BenKosky1) and tell me what you thought.

So, time to express my heartfelt thanks to a number of people. Firstly, the fantastic team at JMD Media, including Michelle Grainger, Matt Limbert and most of all Steve Caron, who first convinced me this book would be worth writing. Like so many, I wasn't sure how to fill the days when the Covid-19 pandemic struck and suddenly everyone found their diaries wiped. Steve's immediate enthusiasm helped me to find a much-needed focus during that strange, unsettling period.

I was absolutely thrilled and honoured when Kevin Gallen agreed to contribute a foreword to the book. Not only is he a QPR legend, a homegrown talent who wore the hooped shirt – and that magic hat – with distinction, but a lifelong Rangers fan who cares deeply about the club. Kevin and his brothers, Joe and Steve, have given so much to QPR over the years and I'm grateful for his contribution to these pages as well.

My thanks also to Dave Brennan, who kindly allowed me to use so many of the photographs he accumulated during our away days following QPR around the country. Given the number of different players who represented the team each season, I'm amazed Dave had sufficient memory on his camera!

I greatly appreciate the support and encouragement offered by friends and acquaintances from around the QPR 'community'. A particular mention to

Richard Jacobs, with whom I've shared many highs and lows as a Rangers fan over the years – and thank you for putting in your time to advise and assist me on publicising the book.

One other person has shared the tribulations of following QPR with me even more closely – apart from the years when I completely lost interest, anyway! My brother, Dan Kosky, has been alongside me for so many memorable Rangers experiences – not too many successes, come to think of it, but I'm grateful for that bond. Thank you Dan – and also for suggesting the title of this book, which I felt was a perfect fit.

# KICK-OFF

Everyone who goes into sports journalism, I imagine, dreams about getting involved with the team they follow. Whether that means reporting on the team or actually working for them directly, the seeds sown during your formative years were nurtured by the experience of watching the team that matters most to you. Love of the sport itself, of course, plays its part – but the idea of being paid to cover your own team? That can alleviate the drudgery of media law and shorthand, add value to those weeks of voluntary work experience – and the months or years of producing content you may not find particularly engaging.

Well, I'm no different. I grew up in Ealing as a Queens Park Rangers fan, a few miles away from the club's Loftus Road ground. My brother and I held season tickets in the Loft Upper Stand behind the goal during the 1990s, when QPR were solidly mid-table (and sometimes higher) in the top division – until one year when they suddenly weren't. And, after dropping out of the Premier League in 1996, they began a rapid slide that culminated in administration and third-tier football.

But of course we stuck with Rangers. As every true football fan knows, you don't give up on your team because times are hard, do you?

That's certainly what I believed fervently at the time, as we shared in the rebirth of our club – hauled back up by the passion and enthusiasm of our manager, Ian Holloway, and a team built around committed players who shared his outlook. The play-off final defeat to Cardiff City in 2003 was heartbreaking – not least because the game took place in Cardiff and panned out as an extremely tight contest, settled by an injury-time goal.

And yet it felt as if that play-off experience had reawakened the collective spirit of Rangers fans, numbed by years of stagnation, paving the way for the memorable promotion season that followed. A full Loftus Road, where the crowd are almost on top of the pitch, generated a magnificent atmosphere and the team responded by holding on to take the runners-up spot, beating Sheffield Wednesday 3-1 on the final day of the season.

Oddly enough, I remember feeling unusually confident as we travelled to Hillsborough that day, and remained so, even when the stadium scoreboard signalled that promotion rivals Bristol City were ahead – and would therefore edge Rangers out if we failed to win. 'Never mind what they're doing, it's all about what we do here,' I told a slightly nervous supporter in the row behind us, attempting to channel my inner Holloway but failing to come up with a suitable simile.

That brazen confidence was rewarded when Kevin Gallen fired Rangers into the lead and Paul Furlong made it 2-0 early in the second half. I'll admit a few waves of doubt washed over me when Wednesday pulled it back to 2-1. But I had a perfect view of the incident that effectively put the game to bed as home defender Chris Carr attempted to clear Martin Rowlands's cross – it was immediately clear that ugly slice was destined to end up in the corner of his own net. And then it was a case of waiting for the final whistle, the raucous cheers, the players' frenzied celebrations that left us in no doubt how much it meant to them. Not only the dyed-in-the-wool QPR supporters like Gallen and Marc Bircham, but all the others who had worked so hard to launch the revival of our club.

Promotion was a new – and slightly surreal – experience for so many of us. I had rarely felt quite so proud and exhilarated to be a QPR fan.

But the next time Rangers won promotion, the emotions I felt would be utterly contrasting. Indifferent? Yes. Saddened? Absolutely. Even slightly nauseated, in fact. Things I could never have envisaged on that triumphant journey back from Sheffield in 2004.

This is how I found myself falling out of love with Queens Park Rangers FC …

# 1

# WAVE OF EMOTION HELPS TO SINK THE HAMMERS

(September 2004)

I really wanted to be a broadcaster rather than a member of the written press. Listening to football commentaries and reports on BBC Radio (sport was on Radio 2 then, accompanied by a distinctive theme tune that later transferred to a new home at 5 Live), it seemed clear to me that Peter Jones, Mike Ingham and Bryon Butler et al had the best job in the world.

And then came Capital Gold – a very different style of broadcasting, built around the notion that all football was relentlessly thrilling – and why speak when you could shout? As many football fans who grew up in London around this time will know, Jonathan Pearce was the chief standard-bearer for this approach. I remember tuning in to Capital Gold's coverage of a QPR game at Highbury, about 20 minutes after kick-off, to be greeted with Pearce in full flow, screeching a series of elongated syllables and words that left me in little doubt he had just witnessed one of the all-time classic goals.

Around five minutes later – when the commentator's exhilaration had abated slightly – I learned that Lee Dixon had just put Arsenal ahead from the penalty spot!

So it was the approach of the BBC Radio reporters, rather than Pearce's, that I gravitated towards when I had a stab at it myself. Hospital radio was the first avenue – it was great fun, even with the realisation that your audience was unlikely to exceed double figures, and sometimes even that might be optimistic. Still, it gave me a taste for broadcasting, the opportunity to talk at length about QPR and a means of getting to know Tony Incenzo – a name the majority of Rangers supporters will recognise instantly.

Tony is something of a club legend. An obsessive Rangers follower since childhood, he is enormously proud of the fact that he never misses a home game without a very, very good reason – the birth of his child being about the only occurrence that falls into that category. His knowledge of the club's history is remarkable and he is utterly passionate about football at all levels, amassing considerable collections of programmes and memorabilia – although, curiously, without taking any interest whatsoever in other sports.

At the time, as well as reporting on matches for the aforementioned Capital Gold, Tony was the voice of QPR Clubcall. In pre-internet days, the Clubcall telephone lines – operating at a premium rate – were the chief source of information about your team, providing updates and interviews as well as ticket news and so on. Tony's radio commitments often meant he needed an additional voice to help with Clubcall commentary at away matches and, to my surprise, he invited me to help out. Maybe he'd been unfortunate enough to be stuck in a hospital bed at some point and tuned in to hear my disjointed ramblings?

Whatever the reason, I was more than happy to join him during the next few seasons at largely unglamorous venues such as Roots Hall, Edgeley Park and the Manor Ground. Ah yes, the Manor Ground. In common with many Rangers fans who witnessed our Wembley horror show against Oxford in the 1986 Milk Cup Final – having knocked out Chelsea and Liverpool to get there – I can't deny that I'd harboured a mild grudge against the men in yellow ever since. Well, I was only ten at the time of our gruesome 3-0 defeat – and at that age you don't realise Wembley appearances may only come around once in a blue moon!

As well as being one of the biggest dumps in professional football, the Manor Ground was also where I witnessed another utterly abysmal display from a QPR side, in September 1998. Oxford won 4-1 to consign Rangers to the bottom of the table, and it fell to me to try and extract some vaguely positive remarks from the Rangers manager, Ray Harford, after the match.

In that respect, I failed as badly as the players had just done. Falling back on the predictable approach of 'what positives can you take from that performance?' or something similar did not bear fruit. Harford, looking every inch a man who would rather be anywhere else, told me, 'Nothing. I don't know what else I can do.'

And off he went to discover that, unlikely as it might have seemed, his day had got even worse and thieves had broken into his car. I can't say Harford's resignation two days later came as an enormous surprise but, with hindsight, his 11 months in charge would one day come to appear lengthy for a QPR manager.

Clubcall eventually morphed into Planet Online – the forerunner of QPR World – as the internet age began to dawn, but the brief remained much the same, dialling in to the appropriate channel and broadcasting live down a telephone line during and after the match. Despite the team's fortunes generally oscillating between bad and worse, there were some memorable games to report on – the 2-2 draw at Maine Road featuring Jamie Pollock's unforgettable own goal that effectively saved Rangers and sent Manchester City down, for instance.

Another memorable 2-2 draw came at Sheffield United, with Steve Morrow's equaliser in the sixth minute of injury time earning QPR an unexpected point. Not that the game itself was a classic – it lodges in my mind because I was fortunate enough to be commentating from the old-fashioned Bramall Lane press box. Old-fashioned because it was located at the very back of the stand, behind glass – cutting you off completely from the crowd noise and creating the uncomfortable feeling that you were talking to yourself. Despite that, I couldn't avoid a certain level of excitement as Morrow stabbed the ball into the net – and, unwisely, thumped the desk in front of me at the same time. The vibration clearly alerted disgruntled Blades fans just in front of the press box, who immediately swung around to … let's say, indicate their displeasure. The upshot being that I had to complete my commentary and sign off while attempting to ignore the contorted, scowling faces and abusive hand gestures that were now heading my way.

Again, one of the drawbacks to reporting on your own team. However, the opportunities to do that began to decrease from around the turn of the millennium, as my career in regional newspapers progressed and I became, if not a member of the claret and blue family at West Ham United, perhaps a temporary lodger.

I ended up working for local papers for a simple reason – it was the first opportunity of full-time work that came my way. Ultimately there comes a point – especially after three years as a student and six months with virtually no income at all – when you have to start paying your way!

The task of reporting on West Ham for the weekly *Recorder* series in east London and Essex fell into my lap, basically. I'd started out as a news reporter at the *Slough Observer*, learning the trade and gradually inching towards the sports desk, but I was always on the lookout for a full-time sports role, and when the *Recorder* advertised a vacancy it seemed to fit the bill. Fortunately the group editor, Tom Duncan, seemed to think I would fit the bill too.

The first six months were chiefly about getting my feet under the table, becoming familiar with the area and its lesser-known sports teams. Covering West Ham was undoubtedly the flagship role, so to speak, and the *Recorder* had strong ties with the club, built up over many years by veteran writer Trevor Smith, Steve Bacon – who held a photographic role with both – and Tom himself.

Frank Praverman, who had taken over from Trevor as Hammers correspondent a few years back, announced he would be moving on to work for *The Sun* in the summer of 2000 – and, to my surprise, Tom immediately decreed that I would take over from him. It was a big call to hand the plum job on the desk to a 24-year-old who hadn't worked there all that long, and I remain grateful to him for showing that faith in me. To the best of my knowledge, there was no consultation or discussion with the sports editor – it was an executive decision and all of a sudden I was being asked to report on a Premier League club.

Frank briefed me on who was who at West Ham and gave me some general bits of advice, including one that has stuck in my mind ever since: 'Make sure you get on with Harry,' he said. 'But don't believe a word he says.'

Harry, of course, was Harry Redknapp. About to begin what turned out to be his final season as West Ham's manager, already well-renowned as one of the game's characters and a huge favourite among the media at large.

I know some people think I don't like Harry Redknapp, but they're mistaken. As a person, it's almost impossible not to like him. Many years later, I was vehemently opposed to the idea of him becoming QPR manager because I knew he was the last thing the club needed at that time. But I have to say that during my first season reporting on West Ham, Harry was very good to me. He'd always make time to speak to me, either over the phone or at the training ground, and even asked on one occasion, as the team bus prepared to depart from an away game, whether I needed a lift home!

In a way, I learned what Harry was all about right from the start, when I went to report on one of their pre-season games at Thurrock. As you'd expect, there were a number of youth-team players named on the team sheet and, having done a bit of research, I knew Izzy Iriekpen was one of the club's promising young centre-backs. So after an impressive performance by the youngster, it seemed worth talking him up when the small clutch of journalists gathered to get some quotes from the West Ham boss after the game.

When I mentioned Iriekpen's performance, however, Harry appeared surprisingly reluctant to discuss the defender. 'Er yeah, he did well, for sure,' was about all I got out of him and, after a few more questions and answers, the small group began to disperse with murmurs of, 'Cheers, Harry'. At that point, with the other journalists now out of earshot, the manager signalled to me that he wanted a quick word.

'Look, don't mention anything about Iriekpen, OK?' Harry began. 'The thing is, that wasn't him. This lad's a triallist – his name's Norman something. I think he's from Zambia. All right? Thought you ought to know!'

And that was Harry Redknapp in a nutshell. Norman – who was never seen again in a West Ham shirt, incidentally – was by no means the only obscure ringer to feature in friendlies under an assumed name! At the same time, I was appreciative of the way Harry had taken the trouble to prevent me looking a total idiot in print.

With that said, I got on best with Harry's successor, Glenn Roeder – and not only because he had once graced the QPR shirt with distinction. I don't think Glenn was ever given a fair go by the media at large – and part of the reason for that was the very fact he had taken over from Redknapp. Suddenly the matey banter and entertaining soundbites had disappeared, to be replaced by someone visibly less at ease in front of the cameras. That was the evidence on which many journalists – and Hammers fans – judged Glenn, but the reality was quite different. Glenn was a lot more relaxed and chatty when I saw him in his office on a Monday morning and, yes, he might not have been the most quotable man in football, but at least you never felt he was trying to lead you up the garden path. He didn't shy away from tricky subjects either – an example being when he explained to me why the club wouldn't offer one of their biggest-name players, Paolo di Canio, a new contract.

Di Canio was the darling of the Hammers fans, keeping them entertained with outrageous skill and confidence on the ball. But maybe you had to be a non-Hammers fan to see what was evident to me – that the team functioned better as a unit without him and that, when it came to away games especially, he played when he wanted to play. I didn't have a problem with reporting and explaining the manager's thinking when it came to Di Canio, although I know it didn't go down too well with several *Recorder* readers.

It was an unpopular view among some of the other 'regulars' in the West Ham media themselves, virtually all of whom bled claret and blue. But I honestly felt that, at times, the fact I wasn't a supporter of the club helped to give me a clearer perspective. Don't get me wrong, I was more than happy to see West Ham doing well – when the club are buzzing and the people around them are generally feeling more positive, they'll be more inclined to chat to the man from the local paper.

The relationship between the club and the paper was so strong that I was even allowed, on one occasion, to accompany West Ham on their chartered flight back from a midweek game at Newcastle. It's strange to think that, at the time, the powers that be at Recorder House – and yes, that was the name of the office – held the view that if West Ham were in action the newspaper had to be represented at the match. If that meant forking out for air travel or an overnight stay, so be it, provided you got the cheapest deal you could. When I pointed out that it would be impossible for me to get back from Tyneside at that time of night, Steve Bacon – who was already on board in his West Ham photographic role – made enquiries to see if they had room for one more. Glenn gave his consent, which I think underlined the fact that he trusted me to keep anything I saw or heard to myself. Given that Newcastle won the game 4-0, it may not seem surprising when I say I can't recall spirits being much higher than 'subdued' among my fellow passengers on the flight back to Stansted.

I did particularly enjoy the fact that there were so many connections between the Hammers and QPR around that time. Glenn's number two was Paul Goddard and the coaching staff also included Roger Cross and Ludek Miklosko, while Les Ferdinand and Rufus Brevett – two of the players I'd enjoyed watching at Loftus Road not too long ago – also found their way to Upton Park in due course and I was able to interview both of them. To be honest, getting to speak to any members of the playing or coaching staff at West Ham was rarely, if ever, a problem – something that football journalists nowadays might find impossible to believe.

True, it helped that West Ham's press officer and programme editor at the time, Peter Stewart, was one of the friendliest and most easy-going people you could hope to meet. Peter would always help if you asked him, but basically he didn't really get involved unless he needed to. I think there was a general assumption that, if you were one of the regulars at West Ham – among the local media, anyway – you'd want to make a positive contribution to the club rather than anything that might paint them in a negative hue. Again, I was perhaps fortunate that, despite being an outsider, I could tap into the stock of goodwill accumulated by my *Recorder* colleagues. Along with phone numbers!

Manager, assistant manager, chief executive, club secretary – their numbers were all in my contacts book and I made frequent use of them to check information and generate stories. So was Michael Carrick's – an emerging prospect at the time, he still lived in a shared house with a few other young professionals and could be contacted via the landline there. Often, though, there was no need to use the phone at all. Nobody was bothered if I approached players or coaching staff at the training ground and asked for a chat. And I do mean myself personally, not a group 'huddle' of journalists as tends to be the case now. That isn't meant to suggest I had some kind of special status, it's just the way things were done around the early 2000s – and had been for decades, I suppose.

What a contrast to the set-up now, not just in the Premier League but at most levels of the game. Everything is now funnelled into a formal, staged press conference, where every single word that drips from a manager's lips is evaluated and analysed incessantly, with many journalists more concerned with being 'seen' to ask a particular question rather than actually finding out useful information. Player interviews? Once in a blue moon, granted only with the press department's say so and sometimes with a few weeks' notice required. Otherwise you can take your chances in the post-match 'mixed zone' – an utterly bizarre phrase that somehow shoehorned its way into the accepted media-speak lexicon. Basically, this consists of a narrow corridor somewhere between the changing rooms and the stadium exit where members of the media loiter, fenced off by a rope or some other kind of barrier, and attempt to persuade players to stop for interviews. Some players will just ignore those entreaties, pretending to be engaged in a phone conversation or listening to music through their outsized headphones. Others will politely – or less politely – decline. And the few who 'stop' then become the object of a frantic media scrum, with quotes-starved journalists rushing to force, perhaps even contort, themselves and their phones or cameras into a position to record the player's observations. All fairly undignified and sometimes not particularly fruitful either.

But the main problem is that, for the vast majority of journalists, it becomes impossible to establish any kind of personal relationship with a player or manager. This used to be vital and I'd suggest that its virtual absence nowadays has certainly had a detrimental effect on the quality of football journalism.

Another point that might seem surprising, viewed through the prism of football today, is that a lot of the players and training ground staff actually read the local paper. I'm not suggesting that Joe Cole, for example, used to pop down to the newsagent's to pick up a copy of the *Recorder* – but he'd certainly glance at one on a Friday, when Steve Bacon and I used to take about a dozen down to the training ground. We'd leave the papers around the canteen for players, coaches and anyone else to leaf through while having their lunch. Even some of the French players read them, as I recall – but I don't remember receiving all that much feedback as a rule.

One exception to that rule came after the Hammers had been thrashed 4-1 by local rivals Millwall. It was an abject performance from the team in claret and blue, to the extent that I was completely stumped when it came to nominating a player for our regular 'Hammer of the Week' slot in the paper. So instead I gave the award to Andy Walker, who was usually the reserve-team physio but had been elevated to first-team duty at The Den and made the observation – a rather sarcastic one, I suppose – that he, at least, hadn't put a foot wrong on derby day.

My verdict didn't go unnoticed by Glenn Roeder's successor as manager, Alan Pardew. A few months into the job, he hadn't yet been able to engineer the kind of consistency in his team that was required to secure a play-off place (West Ham had been relegated with a record points total of 42 the previous season). So he was understandably touchy about that kind of criticism and, having read what I'd written, made a show of stuffing his copy of the newspaper into the nearest bin.

Pardew invited me to 'have a word' in his office. It turned out to be nine words, actually – 'I thought you were taking the piss, quite frankly.'

It appeared unwise to acknowledge that he was spot on there. So I did my best to smooth things over with him and we seemed to get back on track – as did the team, reaching the play-off final at the end of the season. They were beaten by Crystal Palace in a gritty match at Cardiff's Millennium Stadium, best remembered for Pardew's curious decision to substitute his entire trio of forwards at 1-0 down.

West Ham's defeat in Cardiff meant I would be facing an interesting personal challenge the following season – it was just a few weeks earlier that QPR had made certain of promotion to the Championship at Hillsborough. For the first time, the team I was paid to report on would be playing against the team I supported.

As it turned out, the two meetings between West Ham and QPR came in quick succession that autumn and it finished honours even, with Matthew Rose's strike giving Rangers a 1-0 win at Loftus Road and the Hammers hitting back to record a 2-1 victory on their own turf a few weeks later. But the games were both strange experiences for me. I was acutely aware that I couldn't be seen to express too much emotion, especially as many of my regular matchday colleagues were supporting the other team. Writing match reports and reaction pieces on a QPR game – but not from a QPR perspective – also felt weird. Maybe, looking back, those two matches helped nudge me towards the irresistible opportunity that was about to come my way.

Perhaps I've gone into way too much depth about my time reporting on a club that I didn't support. However, there are two reasons for harping on about my involvement with West Ham. The first is to put across some idea of how much I enjoyed doing the job and to stress that an alternative role really needed to be something even more exciting and rewarding to make me give it up. The other aspect of those four and a half years is to try and give a clear impression of what it was like to be a regional newspaper football reporter at that time. The culture I had grown used to was one where you worked to maintain close ties to a club, a relationship that was for the most part mutually beneficial, founded on trust and widely dispensing with formality and protocol.

Towards the end of 2004, Archant – the media company that owned the *Recorder* series – merged with Independent News & Media to create a bigger stable of local newspaper titles, particularly around London. The INM papers included *the Times* series, centred around the boroughs of Brent, Hammersmith and Westminster and which, I noted, had produced an excellent promotion supplement to mark QPR's return to the Championship earlier that year.

Over the years, I'd got to know Dave Evans, who was the sports editor of those titles and oversaw their coverage of QPR with the help of two freelancers, David McIntyre and Noam Friedlander. Both of them were Rangers supporters, whereas Dave made no bones about being a diehard Brentford fan! Despite that, he seemed to enjoy writing about a team he actively disliked for personal reasons. Brentford fans of a particular vintage have never forgiven QPR for the aborted attempt to buy their Griffin Park ground in the 1960s, but as the two clubs' paths had rarely crossed during the next 35 years, it was a rivalry largely lost on my generation.

However, Dave lived in Essex and the merger had forced him to relocate to the company's office in Swiss Cottage – something of a logistical nightmare in terms of commuting. So he and the new head of group sport, Trevor Davies, put a proposal to me. A job swap, which would kill two birds with one stone. Dave could work at an office much closer to home … and what was in it for me?

I'd also be based closer to home. I'd now be in charge of the sports content for my own papers, something I hadn't previously experienced. And I'd be paid to report on QPR.

How could I possibly refuse?

# 2

# PRIDE AND PASSION ARE THIS YEAR'S PLUS POINTS

## (May 2005)

The answer to my question was, of course, self-evident. Although I didn't say yes straight away to the proposed job swap – doing my best to weight up the pros and cons objectively – I knew I would always regret it if I passed up the opportunity of taking on a role that brought me closer to my club. Although I was only 29 and, in theory at least, still had all the time in the world to realise this ambition, there was no guarantee the chance would ever come around again. No need to put in an application or prepare for an interview – this was mine if I wanted it.

It wasn't just about seeking to be someone that fellow QPR fans would read, or listen to on a regular basis. I also saw it as an opportunity for me to help the club out, in some small way. The ethos that had developed at Loftus Road in recent years – spearheaded, I would say, by our inspirational manager – was one of everyone pulling together. Players, fans and everyone with some interest in QPR doing their bit to drag a penniless club back towards a higher status. My experiences at the *Recorder* had taught me that a local paper could play its part in that as well.

I met Dave for a chat after Rangers' 1-0 win against Stoke in January 2005 and we thrashed out some details of how, and when, the switch would work. This wasn't only, I should stress, about QPR and West Ham – it was also about familiarising ourselves with all the other teams and sports we would both need to get to grips with. Non-league football, cricket, athletics, boxing, rugby, bowls … there was plenty to take in and also some time needed to introduce ourselves to the people involved with those sports on the new 'patch'.

Coincidentally, my final West Ham player interview was with Bobby Zamora, who would go on to score the play-off final winner that secured their return to the Premier League in May – and would, of course, repeat that achievement in a Rangers shirt nine years later. Still, it was Dave who got to cover the Hammers' promotion success while I had to make do with an 11th-place finish!

No complaints whatsoever, though – I was loving my new role. I'd maintained some contact with the media side of things at Loftus Road, helping out with the QPR World commentary now and then when the fixture list worked out the right way, so I already knew the club's chief press officer, Phil Harris, and his colleagues Billy Rice and Jackie Bass. Billy introduced me properly to Ian Holloway on my first visit to the training ground in Acton and I found straight away that what you saw from Ollie was what you got, whether that was joking around and frivolity or being deadly serious and impassioned about a subject. The QPR manager was definitely in the former mood when we approached the pitch that morning – using a bright orange training cone to simulate a former team-mate getting his tackle out, as he loudly proclaimed to all and sundry. I felt straight away we were likely to get on!

As well as meeting the manager, I got to chat to Lee Cook and also did a piece with the goalkeeping coach Tony Roberts about our former keeper Nick Culkin, who had just been forced to retire through injury. As had been the case with West Ham, arranging interviews was usually straightforward and that was how it remained over the next two or three years.

The team were more than holding their own in the Championship, enough to keep hopes of a play-off charge alive going into April, although injuries meant they fell away during those final weeks. But the flip side of that was something I viewed in a positive light and I'm sure many other fans did too – the fact that younger lads like Stefan Bailey and Shabazz Baidoo were getting some first-team experience in those games. Given the financial state of the club, it didn't seem remotely likely that QPR would find themselves in a position to discard rather than nurture young talent at any time in the near future.

I did manage to get to a handful of Rangers' away games during the remainder of the season, but there was a change from what I'd been used to in that you were no longer expected to attend every match. The general rule of thumb post-merger was, if you can get there and back by claiming £50 or less in expenses, all well and good. Any more than that and questions would be asked! This was probably why my colleagues who reported on the likes of Arsenal, Tottenham and Chelsea tended to 'opt out' of away matches outside the capital, safe in the knowledge that either full coverage or highlights were easily available on TV. What I also learned – to my surprise as it contrasted with my experiences at West Ham – was that none of the blokes covering those Premier League clubs were given much at all in terms of access to players. So it really wasn't worth their while to charge around the country watching every game and trying to stay within that £50 budget.

My perspective, at this stage, was still very different. Firstly, as a QPR supporter, I was keen to see the team in action as often as possible. But it was also about trying to accumulate brownie points with the players and the management – being 'seen' as that guy who would make the effort to turn up at Deepdale, Turf Moor or Carrow Road rather than just at home. So, by and large, I decided I would aim to be at the majority of games when the new season began in August.

Until then, I needed to try and keep my finger on the Loftus Road pulse. With no matches taking place over the summer, that meant regular telephone calls to Ollie, as well as Bill Power, the QPR chairman. I was aware that Dave had enjoyed a strong relationship with the chairman and hoped to maintain that. Bill was a thoroughly genial guy and, even if I caught him in a meeting or having lunch, he would always call back later and try to steer me in the right direction. Bill confirmed that the club were interested in signing a couple of ex-Chelsea players – Dennis Wise and Tore Andre Flo – although, as it turned out, neither of those ever materialised.

Several other players did arrive at Loftus Road that summer, however. It seemed like several at the time, although in subsequent years nine new signings would come to represent more of a trickle than a flood. What was gradually becoming apparent to me, though, was that the manager's views on transfer targets didn't always have much bearing on the identity of the new faces who eventually showed up at the training ground.

Left-back, for example, looked like an area that needed addressing following the club's about-turn concerning Gino Padula. A key member of Rangers' promotion-winning side, the popular Argentinian had originally been promised a new contract, only to end up leaving the club instead. So it was common knowledge that Ollie was on the lookout for a new left-back and, for the first time, I attempted to get involved in making a transfer happen! I knew that Chris

Powell, the former England defender, was out of contract at West Ham and also knew, from previous conversations with him, that he might be interested in playing for QPR.

'Yeah, of course I'd like to speak to him,' said Ollie. 'What you could do for me is pass on his phone number.'

I rummaged in my little black book – and no, it's not a cliché, I really did write down phone numbers in a little black book – and found Powell's details. I honestly thought he'd be just what the team needed, so I really hoped something might come of it.

Those hopes, unfortunately, fizzled out into a damp squib when it turned out Powell must have changed his number! So bang went any ambitions I might have harboured of becoming a football agent, Powell opted to rejoin Charlton anyway – and Ollie ended up with a former Italy international named Mauro Milanese instead.

'He's here on a six-month contract,' Ollie told me, and I've no doubt he believed that information to be accurate. As it turned out, Milanese had been signed for a year – and not by the manager. Ollie was similarly vague about the details of another summer arrival, the 6ft 5in Danish centre-forward Marc Nygaard, who moved to Rangers on a free transfer from Brescia. The Italian connection certainly wasn't a coincidence. Milanese and Nygaard were among numerous players brought to Loftus Road by Gianni Paladini, the former agent who was now on the board as part of the Monaco-based consortium that had invested in the club a couple of years earlier. I hadn't met Paladini at that time, but he would soon become an extremely familiar figure to me and many other Rangers fans.

One player who certainly was on the Rangers manager's wish list ahead of the 2005-06 season was his fellow Bristolian, City's combative midfielder Tommy Doherty. His arrival at Loftus Road really underlined the importance of how a good relationship between the club and the local press ought to work – and that was all thanks to Phil Harris.

One of the problems I faced, and no doubt it was the same for every other journalist on a weekly newspaper at that time, was the issue of print deadlines. In the case of *the Times* series, a Wednesday publication – although it later moved to Thursday – that meant all the sports pages had to be dispatched to the production department by 3pm on Tuesday. This was far from ideal given the number of Championship matches that took place on a Tuesday night. Apart from the obvious absence of match details in the paper, there was always the risk that the subject of your headline story might have picked up an injury or suspension in that game, rendering their comments very much out of date before they'd even appeared on the shelves at the local newsagent's!

On top of that, another potential pitfall was that a major story could develop on a Tuesday afternoon – which again could make all the previous week's hard work look stale and jaded through no fault of your own. It's important to be clear, as well, that newspaper websites were still in their infancy at this stage and many journalists just didn't have the tools to keep them looking fresh all the time. Maybe it's just that Archant were typically behind the game, but none of us even had laptops until a few years later.

Anyway, the good news for me was that Phil understood all this – and, having learned that the Doherty signing was due to go through on a Tuesday afternoon, he phoned me up that morning to make sure we could include the story. To me, that spoke volumes about Phil's professionalism and realisation that you couldn't take a uniform approach to 'the media' – local newspapers have different needs and requirements to nationals. And there was an unspoken trust there as well – firstly, he trusted us not to blab news of Doherty's transfer to fans' forums or anything similar. Second, he trusted us to reciprocate in future if he needed publicity that the club might not get elsewhere – a story about a QPR in the Community scheme, for example. You scratch my back, I'll scratch yours. I don't see anything wrong with that approach as a general rule of thumb.

Phil was also very good at managing situations that might develop. On another occasion, for instance, I'd printed some remarks from Ollie hinting QPR might ignore the transfer window, which was a relatively new concept and unpopular with a number of clubs below Premier League level. Having read the story, Phil rang me up and politely asked me to let him know if the manager sounded off about this kind of thing in future, simply because it was a sensitive subject within football politics and he'd rather have some say in how it was reported. I had no problem with that whatsoever – I didn't see it as a case of interference with the press, but an effort to avoid getting QPR into unnecessary hot water with the football authorities. Again, I felt at the time my job was primarily to help the club rather than challenge them – and it's worth stressing that because of the way I ended up revising my outlook a few years down the line.

I was sorry to see Phil leave QPR about a year into my role, but he had the chance to return 'home' to Norfolk and work in local government communications, which wasn't a bad gig – and probably a more secure position given some of the extraordinary occurrences that were now beginning to unfold at Loftus Road.

Few more extraordinary, it must be said, than the off-field events which surrounded and overshadowed Rangers' second home game of the season. Reports that Gianni had been threatened at gunpoint in the boardroom began to circulate soon after the 2-1 victory over Sheffield United. Truthfully, there isn't a great deal I can add to what was extensively said and alleged at the time, eventually leading to six men standing trial and being cleared of all charges the following year. I recall seeing Gianni appear at the top of the steps that led to the directors' box, just after Marc Bircham had put Rangers ahead early in the second half. Two things struck me as strange – firstly that Gianni was visibly in tears as he celebrated the goal and also that he was accompanied by a uniformed policeman.

The atmosphere after the game was somewhat weird as everyone tried to piece together what had actually happened, and there's no question that the team's excellent start to the season – seven points out of a possible nine – had been virtually forgotten. I rang Bill on the Monday morning to see if he had any comment to make and he declined, saying he was too upset by what had happened.

That was the last time I spoke to Bill in his capacity as QPR chairman. Just over a week later, he was voted out by Gianni and his allies on the board, with chief executive Mark Devlin fired at the same time. Gianni took over as the new chairman and also incorporated the CEO role into his duties. It was widely reported as a 'coup' and I suppose that remains the best way of describing what took place. One thing was clear from my point of view – whereas up to then Gianni had seemed to be a peripheral figure, now he was unquestionably the main mover and shaker at Loftus Road and someone I needed to try and get to know.

Meanwhile, despite my failure to help bring Chris Powell on board, I did get involved with another transfer before the deadline passed at the end of the month. This time I got wind of Rangers' interest in signing another West Ham player, Steve Lomas – someone I knew fairly well as he'd written a weekly column for the *Recorder* over the past few seasons. When I say written, I mean the column was put together in the way these things usually are – the journalist would speak to the player to get his thoughts and then write the column, keeping the style and content as close to his original words as possible. So I rang him up to find out whether he'd actually agreed the move to Loftus Road – he pretty much had, anyway – but I did my best to offer encouragement and sing the club's praises all the same, in case of any lingering doubts.

Lomas signed on the same day as another midfielder, Richard Langley – who in this case was rejoining Rangers for a second spell after two seasons at Cardiff. Curiously enough, Langers would later become a columnist for us himself, although he was the exception to the rule in that he did actually compile the column himself and email it over. It was always a good read, too, which made it little more than a copy and paste job for me!

The introduction of a regular player column was something I'd decided to try in *the Times* series from the start of that season. The format seemed to work well, provided the author (or the official author, anyway) met three criteria. One, it had to be someone who played regularly in the team – there's only so much mileage to be gained from chatting about reserve-team football or rehab sessions. Two, it had to be someone who spoke well and confidently, who could give honest opinions about the game and didn't communicate in clichés. Finally, and perhaps most importantly, it had to be someone you could get hold of relatively easily! So without too much generalisation, the more experienced players were your best bet for this type of role, ideally family men who were more likely to be at home in the afternoons or evenings. The younger, single players tended to be a little harder to track down …

So for me the obvious choice among the QPR playing staff had to be Marc Bircham. Anyone who wore his support for the club on his sleeve – or, in Birch's case, in his blue-and-white streaked hair – had to be a guaranteed source of good humour, dressing-room banter and general entertainment value. That was pretty much how it turned out to be with Birch, there was always the opportunity to reference players and games from the past because he knew exactly what I was talking about. Sometimes, though, we'd digress from football matters altogether – for instance, his unexpected alarm call when the Buncefield oil depot just down the road from the Bircham family home exploded early one morning.

I remember the build-up to Rangers' game at Stoke that season made interesting reading as Birch was something of a hate figure among Stoke fans, following an incident which resulted in Gerry Taggart's sending off the previous year. In the event, he missed the game but the atmosphere at the Britannia Stadium was no less heated, with Stoke having a player sent off again and Langley hitting the winner from the penalty spot as Rangers triumphed 2-1. The toxic environment eventually exploded Buncefield-style at the final whistle when a group from the home end burst onto the pitch to attack the QPR goalkeeper, Simon Royce.

Overall, that result proved to be a rare highlight during the autumn and early winter months as the team failed to build on their August form. Might it have been a different story, but for that significant off-field distraction? Perhaps. Although they did struggle for consistency, Rangers still looked fairly solid in mid-table, but the greater concern seemed to be that all was not well between board and manager.

Ollie had become renowned as one of the game's more zany characters on the back of what became known as the 'thanks very much, let's have coffee' discourse during the promotion season, when he reflected on a scrappy Rangers victory by comparing it to a night out on the pull. I'm glad to say I was treated to a number of similarly weird and wacky comparisons, my favourite being when the manager was trying to explain the difficulty of making sure you got proper value for money in the transfer market.

'It's like when I've got a leak in my house and I need to call a plumber,' Ollie observed. 'He might spend all day in the house fixing that leak, or he might get the job done in 20 minutes. But I've still got to pay him just the same.'

In all honesty, I didn't really understand the point he was making – and I still don't! But the overall message was clear – the Rangers manager was becoming frustrated when he wasn't able to bring in players he wanted and equally frustrated by having players he didn't want foisted on him.

Ollie could be hilarious even when he was hopping mad. On one visit to the training ground – the club having by now moved to the Imperial College facilities at Harlington – I witnessed him laying into one of the players for messing around during a training exercise. Although the proximity of Heathrow Airport meant you could sometimes hardly hear yourself think, the manager's unmistakeable West Country tones rang out loud and clear.

'You f***ing c***!' he began. 'Do that again and I will f***ing send you indoors!' And then came the best bit. 'Why don't you take your brain out of your head and make it into an omelette?'

Tim Breacker, Gary Penrice and the other coaches looked mildly uncomfortable as they shuffled their feet and looked away, trying not to laugh, but I suppose they just regarded it as part of a normal day in the life of Ian Holloway and Queens Park Rangers.

With injuries leaving him short in attack, Ollie was pondering a move for Barry Hayles, who he had managed earlier in his career at Bristol Rovers, but that idea gained little support in the boardroom. Instead, he put centre-back Georges Santos up front for a home match against Coventry, with little success as the visitors scored a late penalty to take all three points. The Rangers forward line looked equally toothless during the next game, a Boxing Day defeat at Brighton – the only time I visited the Seagulls' woefully inadequate temporary home at the Withdean Stadium.

To be truthful, I knew the day was unlikely to end well for QPR once I saw the name of Rob Styles listed as the match official. Styles was one of those referees who always appeared to be brimming with self-importance and his involvement usually spelt disaster for Rangers in particular. Only an official who made the occasion all about himself would show a straight red card to a teenager ten minutes into his league debut, rather than having a quiet word with the manager or captain to calm him down. Midfielder Marcus Bean had been the victim in question a few years earlier – although he was by no means alone, with a total of four players sent off by Styles that day at Wycombe.

To my surprise, the referee actually retained a full complement of players on this occasion, not that it made much difference to the outcome. I watched that game from the stands as, shortly before kick-off, one gentleman from a national newspaper had managed to throw up in the tiny, eight-seat structure that passed for a press box. Perhaps he was also reacting to the sight of Styles's name on the team sheet, I couldn't be sure – but, although the stadium cleaners did their best to mop up, I thought it might be wise to forgo my seat and stand out in the open space. It was also hard not to feel sorry for the Sky Sports reporter whose company-branded puffer jacket was now spattered with remnants of the previous day's Christmas dinner as he yelled angrily, 'Get him out of here before he does it again!'

While Ollie could be enormously entertaining, I was learning that the club's new chairman was also something of a character. I'd had some communications with Nick de Marco, a barrister who specialised in sports law and was close to

Gianni, and through him I was able to arrange a face-to-face meeting. This, I discovered, was the way Gianni operated – he was open and hospitable, there was certainly no question of arranging this kind of thing through the press office. I spoke to the chairman on what had previously been Mark Devlin's phone at the stadium and he invited me to come up to his office. Simple as that and, once again, the kind of informality that just wouldn't exist today between a football club and a local paper.

I thought I'd better dig out a smart shirt and trousers for the occasion, although I was never likely to match up to the tailored Italian suits sported by Gianni and his fellow Neapolitan, Antonio Caliendo, who was also now a director. When I arrived, Gianni invited me to have some of the Italian delicatessen food they were tucking into, which was a clear indicator he knew the best way to charm journalists. Feed them well and your press coverage is likely to be more favourable!

Even after this effusive welcome, what Gianni did next was utterly astounding. He said, 'You know, some people think we're paying big wages, more than we can afford. But we're doing it sensibly, see yourself.' With that, the chairman opened a drawer in his desk, took out a folder and unearthed a bundle of papers stapled together.

It was the wage bill for the QPR playing staff. Every single member of the first-team squad was listed, along with a figure detailing their weekly salary!

I could hardly believe the chairman was prepared to show me, somebody he barely knew, information about who was earning what at the club. But the point he wanted to make was a sound one – there were no figures anyone could consider extravagant by Championship standards at the time.

It wasn't my place to reveal those figures and I won't do so even now. However, I couldn't help noticing that one member of the squad was earning even less than me! In all honesty, though, fans who witnessed this player's handful of appearances in a Rangers shirt might actually have concluded that I was the better footballer. Years later, I discovered that the player in question had been promised an expensive watch after signing for the club – but I'd be surprised if it ever found its way onto his wrist.

Some of Gianni's comments during the 'on-record' part of our meeting were particularly memorable. I've never forgotten his description of striker Dean Sturridge, who had joined the club with a CV that included impressive spells at

Derby and Wolves, but spent most of his Rangers career out injured. 'When you cut open the melon, it's not always nice and red inside.'

I also asked Gianni if he envisaged the club moving away from Loftus Road in the long term – and his response could just as easily have come from the manager, albeit with a wildly different accent. 'If you've got no money and you're driving a Mini, you always see someone in a Rolls Royce and you wish you could buy that. When I go to Southampton, Leicester and Coventry, then I come to White City and I see workmen building, I wish they were building a new Loftus Road.

'So the alternative would be to move, but it must not be far away. The moment you move QPR to a different area, there's no more QPR and then it's just like Wimbledon. This club has a fantastic history and I cannot change all this by moving the club to Hyde Park. It's a lovely park, but I don't think you can play football there.'

Not surprisingly, I lapped it all up. And yet, despite Gianni's assurance that he backed Ollie '100 per cent', it was still hard to shake the feeling that sooner or later there would come to be a parting of the ways.

Results initially picked up again after the Boxing Day defeat, with home wins against Cardiff and Southampton sandwiching a 4-3 thriller at Crewe, although Rangers were unsurprisingly knocked out of the FA Cup at the first hurdle. When I say it came as no surprise, I've taken into account not only that a third-round tie away to Premier League opposition in Blackburn was always likely to be difficult, but simply that any QPR fan's expectations of an FA Cup run around this time would be zero. It must be said that Rangers were spectacularly woeful in this competition during Ollie's tenure – and, for that matter, his second spell in charge as well. They failed to win a single game and racked up a roll-call of ignominy that included Grimsby, MK Dons and, most embarrassing of all, Vauxhall Motors.

With the January transfer window open, players continued to seep into Loftus Road at a rapid rate. Ollie had wanted a striker and he ended up with two – neither of whom were much good. Danish forward Sammy Youssouf made six appearances without scoring, while Leon Clarke, one of two players to sign on loan from Wolves, was so poor that it remains a mystery to me how he ended up signing permanently for QPR a few years later. Then there was Poland international defender Marcin Kus, who played only a handful of games and, most bizarrely of all, a one-match loan deal for Sheffield United goalkeeper Phil Barnes.

Kus and Barnes both made their debuts in what transpired to be Ollie's final game in charge, a 2-0 defeat away to Leeds. But it was the previous match that sticks in my memory, when Leicester snatched a late 3-2 victory at Loftus Road, and the manager turned up in the press room afterwards to give his reaction. Nothing unusual in that, of course. What was strange was that, whereas normally Ollie – and everyone else – would be keen to head home after a midweek match, this time he remained for more than half an hour after the on-record stuff had concluded, just chatting with the regulars, maybe five or six of us. I don't recall specific details of the conversation, but it mostly amounted to Ollie pouring his heart out – a general weariness and unhappiness with the direction the club was taking. I left the ground with the distinct impression that Ollie's days at QPR were numbered.

Ironically, of course, it turned out that the link with Leicester, who had parted company with Craig Levein a week earlier, would be the trigger for Ollie's departure from Loftus Road. On the Monday after the defeat at Leeds, a club statement popped up in my inbox, announcing that he had been 'placed on gardening leave', along with Breacker and Penrice, while Gary Waddock would take over as caretaker manager.

It was a sad and undignified end. As a journalist, my immediate task was to find someone who might have Waddock's phone number to hand. But, as a QPR fan, I felt Ollie's time in charge demanded some kind of public recognition.

Until then, I'd tended to stick with reporting news stories and running interviews. This was the first time I'd tried to put together some kind of comment piece for the paper, conveying my personal opinion instead of someone else's. I cast my mind back over the past five years, recalling the despair of relegation and the Vauxhall Motors game, the emotional highs and lows of the play-offs and the exhilaration of success at Hillsborough. This was how I summed up my thoughts on that Wednesday's back page:

*Holloway, whose spell as manager spanned nearly five years, was the longest-serving QPR boss since Alec Stock in the 1960s, and his contribution to the club's history was probably just as significant.*

*It is no exaggeration to say that QPR might have folded without Holloway's infectious enthusiasm and passion to haul the club back from the twin blows of relegation and administration in 2001.*

*And, while the manager had come under fire this season after a series of indifferent results and limited success in the transfer market, the way that Holloway restored Rangers' pride and self-belief in recent years should never be underestimated.*

Never mind five years – Ollie's successors would feel they had done extremely well if they completed one! The 'change of manager' template would be given plenty of airings by QPR's press department in the years ahead and I'd find a lot more opportunities to print opinions as the club gradually descended into chaos and farce.

# 3

# WADDOCK ROLE STILL UNCERTAIN

### (September 2006)

In terms of managing QPR, Gary Waddock could have been the right man at the wrong time. That's my honest belief when it comes to assessing his brief time in charge at Loftus Road. He did a magnificent job helping to nurture talented youngsters such as Scott Donnelly and Ray Jones and those strengths would surely have been utilised far more, say ten or 12 years down the line, when it belatedly dawned on the people who ran the club that they needed to start living within their means. Gary was well liked as a coach and he went on to enjoy a certain degree of success as a manager at Aldershot and Wycombe, so it wasn't as if that role was beyond his capability.

Personally, I found him very easy to deal with. There was no side to Gary. Yes, he wasn't as quotable as Ollie had been – although not too many are – but he was always approachable and honest in his opinions, very much like I'd found Glenn Roeder to be at West Ham. I think it also helped that he'd been a popular QPR player in the era I was growing up, so he could relate to the club's values and understand comparisons with the past. On a similar subject, Gary's decision to bring Alan McDonald back to the club as his second in command brought fans onside in a big way. If there was one player who had epitomised dedication to the cause during QPR's 13-year spell in the top flight, it was Macca, a centre-back who was hard as nails, a natural leader and someone who knew just how to deal with the more physical brand of striker. For me, it was an absolute joy to see one of my football heroes back at Loftus Road, fag in hand and happy to impart a yarn or two from his playing days.

When I first spoke to Gary about his new role, he said, 'We need to pick up points, but I want to do it in a style that's entertaining and enjoyable for the players. That's my aim.'

Those were his actual words, but I think they were reported inaccurately elsewhere. It was certainly interpreted by Ollie as a criticism of the football his team had produced and that perceived slight seemed to fester, right up until the following season when Rangers came up against his new club, Plymouth. I genuinely don't believe Gary meant it in that way.

Technically, Gary wasn't appointed manager until the end of the season – because Ollie was still officially the incumbent until he found another job. But there was never any question about the new man's eventual elevation. Gianni was effusive in his backing for the caretaker manager, although he had unsuccessfully tried to persuade former QPR manager Jim Smith, a personal friend, to return in a director of football role.

Initially, at least, Gianni's support for Gary Waddock was borne out by results on the field, with the first three games post-Ollie including wins over Millwall and Sheffield United and some solid performances in the next four, all of which were drawn. Unfortunately, by the time April came around, Rangers' season was all but dead and, after losing six of the final seven games, they eventually finished one place above the bottom three. Particularly galling was the Easter Monday trip to Carrow Road, when the visitors threw away a two-goal lead to lose 3-2 – recalling memories of the same scoreline exactly 30 years earlier, which had ultimately cost QPR their best chance of becoming champions of England.

Meanwhile, I learned that our columnist had been put up for sale. Marc Bircham was among a cluster of senior players to be informed the club would listen to offers for his services that summer – although, given the circumstances, he was actually quite restrained when I called him that week. At least Birch had retained his sense of humour, putting in a bid at the QPR Player of the Year awards night when a place in next season's squad was being auctioned!

I actually attended the event that year, for the first and only time so far, after receiving an invitation. Yes, the A-list status that comes with writing for a local newspaper … or, more truthfully, being asked by my friend Geraldine Field, who worked at the club, to help make up a table at the Hilton Metropole. I didn't mind – it was nice to be there and feel like part of the QPR family, even if some of the players who'd just been placed on the transfer list might not be feeling quite the same. The wine flowed and Danny Shittu deservedly won the Player of the Year award. I was pleased for Big Dan, who was our most consistent defender by far and clearly destined for a shot at the Premier League. He was also refreshingly candid in interviews, as I'd first discovered in my early days at the *Recorder* when I'd written a feature about some of East London's up-and-coming sports stars. He was a teenager at the time, on Charlton's books, but rather than gushing about football, he told me about his interest in computer technology.

More recently, I'd made a beeline for Dan at the training ground one day, hoping to speak to him and preview an upcoming match against Stoke. I can't recall who would have been playing up front for the Potters at the time, but presumably I mentioned a few names and asked Dan how he planned to keep them quiet. A predictable response might have been some general platitudes about the men in question being good players and the need to be 'on our game' or something of that kind. All a bit bland, I suppose, but it helps to fill column inches.

Instead, Dan just started laughing, which wasn't actually that unusual – he's one of those guys who seems to crack up quite easily. 'I don't know much about either of them,' he eventually admitted. 'To be honest, I don't really follow football! I might see *Match of the Day* now and then but that's it.'

I loved his frank admission – and when you think about it, that's a perfectly reasonable reply! We tend to assume footballers are all as obsessed as we are by the game they play, but when all's said and done, why shouldn't they regard it as a job and no more? After all, nobody expects the people who collect plastic and paper for recycling to be fascinated by the latest developments in environmental technology.

Gianni had made it clear that the club would listen to offers for Danny Shittu and the saga of his transfer to Watford, who had just been promoted, dragged on throughout the summer. But there was plenty else for the chairman to talk about – which was why he invited me to 'come up and see him' again soon after the end of the season. Apparently, there were some exciting new players on their way to Loftus Road.

'People think we've been asleep, but it's not true, we've been working hard,' Gianni began, scrolling up his computer screen to bring up details of Nick Ward, the Australian midfielder, on a FIFA page that listed him among the best young prospects in world football. And then he switched to another web page that introduced me to the name Armel Tchakounte.

If any single player epitomised QPR's shambolic recruitment policy around that time, it had to be Armel. The chairman assured me that he would be Rangers' answer to Patrick Vieira or Pape Bouba Diop, who anchored Fulham's midfield and was nicknamed 'The Wardrobe', on account of his bulk and physical presence. The only resemblance Armel bore to a wardrobe, as would become clear, was that he was immobile and had little, if any, resale value. I saw him play in a pre-season friendly at Gillingham and then later for the reserves and, even to my untrained eye, it was evident he was utterly out of his depth. Because of the relatively small attendances at reserve games, it's much easier to hear what's being said on the pitch. On that occasion, it was impossible not to hear the unmistakeable Ulster accent of Steve Lomas bellowing 'For f***s sake, Armel!' as yet another overhit pass ballooned over the touchline.

But the ridiculous thing was Armel's deficiencies should have been evident from his CV. He'd come from Cameroon and played in Hong Kong before joining Carshalton Athletic. On the face of it, no reason why the club shouldn't have been looking at Conference South players, they'd had success in drafting youngsters from a similar level in the past. But Armel certainly wasn't a youngster – officially he was 27 and even that figure, I later discovered, was heavily disputed by some of his new team-mates.

Gianni also explained that the squad would be heading to his neck of the woods during pre-season, playing two games against lower-league teams in the Naples area. Apparently he hadn't been impressed by the previous summer's preparations, when Rangers competed in – and won – the Ibiza Cup tournament, and felt this would be more effective in sharpening the players ahead of a gruelling Championship campaign. Fortunately it didn't occur to me to try and get to Italy when the tour came around, because what I would have witnessed were late changes of venue and opposition, four-hour round trips to reach training sessions, appalling pitches, and Tony Roberts and Alan McDonald coming out of retirement to make up the numbers.

Before QPR got down to the nitty-gritty of pre-season, however, it was a World Cup summer – and hopes were high that England might be able to better their quarter-final performance of 2002 in Japan and South Korea. In common with regional newspaper groups all over the country, Archant quite rightly viewed the tournament as a good opportunity to boost their advertising revenue by producing a supplement across all titles ahead of the big kick-off in Germany. Obviously, though, the clutch of adverts from pubs, sportswear manufacturers, health food outlets and so on had to be flavoured with some editorial content, which meant some brainstorming before working out who got to do the big-name feature interviews and who got to research the Angola squad.

Everyone across the sports department was expected to produce one or two unique 'local' angles on the tournament – not a straightforward assignment for me as, sadly, QPR weren't exactly over-represented in Germany. I settled for a piece with Gerry Francis, the manager who had given Peter Crouch his Rangers debut, and was well-placed to assess the beanpole centre-forward's prospects of making an impact for England.

All seemed to be in order – until, a few days before publication, I caught sight of the design for the supplement cover. To my horror, the main image was that of England defender John Terry – the Chelsea captain and, for most Rangers fans, surely the least popular member of Sven-Goran Eriksson's squad. Being entirely honest, I might not have raised an eyebrow if it had been another Chelsea player such as Frank Lampard – but anyone who knows me is well aware that Terry, in my view, has always been beyond the pale and should never, ever, have been honoured with the captaincy of his country.

I contacted one of the graphic designers straight away. 'Seriously mate, we can't run that in these papers,' I told him. 'Any chance you can sort out an image of another England player instead?'

The guy was more amused than anything else, I suspect, but I asked my editor, Tim Cole, to back me up anyway and he was happy to oblige. It probably helped that Tim had grown up as a Leeds fan, with no love for Chelsea whatsoever, and fully appreciated the problem! I know some of my colleagues thought I was making a fuss about nothing, but to me it was totally unthinkable to market ourselves as a newspaper that focussed on QPR and at the same time run a World Cup supplement festooned with an image of Terry. Fortunately the designer came up with a perfectly acceptable alternative cover, featuring David Beckham instead, and we managed to swerve what I think would have been a major faux pas!

One of the nice aspects of the summer break is that there are often opportunities to attend different football-related events and speak to people you wouldn't otherwise meet. I can't actually recall the event in question where I got to speak to Les Ferdinand – it was probably some kind of PR campaign – but I won't deny feeling at least slightly starstruck! This was the guy I'd watched banging in goals left, right and centre as he transformed from non-league centre-forward to England international and he was someone who clearly still held a place in his heart for QPR.

Interestingly, Les spoke about his possible involvement with a consortium bidding to take over the club and raised the prospect of him returning to Loftus

Road in a director's role! So, in a sense, I suppose I could claim to have broken the story about ten years before it actually happened. A similar story we reported that summer – Rangers' interest in signing Karl Henry from Stoke – also came to fruition many years later, although by then he was primarily a midfielder rather than a right-back. For the time being, though, the club were predictably drawing a blank when it came to landing their top transfer targets and, equally predictably, ending up with alternatives who were fairly average at best.

Polish striker Adam Czerkas, who joined Rangers that summer, fell into that category. From what I saw of him, he didn't seem to offer much up front in terms of presence, pace, control or shooting. It seemed incredible that – given the sizeable Polish community in and around west London – QPR never managed to pick up the kind of player who might have helped to attract some new fans to Loftus Road. Winger Pawel Wszolek helped to redress that balance about ten years later, but there was little chance of Czerkas getting many supporters, Polish or otherwise, on the edge of their seats.

Before the new season got under way, I also needed to find a new columnist. Although Birch had been brilliant in that role, the problem was that he remained transfer-listed and I didn't want a situation where we suddenly had a gaping hole to fill if he moved on. As it happened, Birch later came off the transfer list and stayed for the rest of the season, but at the time it would have been a big risk to take.

Gareth Ainsworth was the man I had earmarked to take over and, in fact, when I asked the manager's permission, he said, 'He's exactly who I would have suggested.' Again, Gareth ticked all the boxes as far as I could see, he had plenty to say about the game and, while he wasn't a QPR fan, his commitment to the cause was never remotely in doubt. He was also well known for his love of rock and roll, so we could help out with publicising his band, Dog Chewed the Handle, and try and get a few Rangers supporters along to their gigs.

As it happened, Gareth turned out to be even more professional than I'd anticipated. The paper had now moved to a Wednesday morning print deadline, which enabled us to include coverage of a Tuesday night game, but it made life a lot easier if I could get everything else on the page beforehand. However, the obvious danger with finishing Gareth's column prior to the Tuesday game was that he might score the winner – not that I'd have complained about that! – or something else of significance could happen. A big win or defeat, or maybe a controversial penalty decision, would need some kind of reference in his column.

'No problem,' said Gareth. 'We'll do most of it beforehand, then just call me again after the game. If it's an away game we'll have a word while I'm getting on the team bus.'

So that was the routine during the next two and a bit years, and I'm sure Gareth would have continued for even longer as our columnist, but for unforeseen circumstances. Namely, him being asked to become QPR caretaker-manager at that point!

Unlikely though it might seem these days, Archant did pay an annual fee for the newspaper column back then – and Gareth asked us to donate it to the Jack Tizard School for children with learning difficulties. The school, which adjoins Loftus Road, also serves as the players' car park on matchdays and, not only did Gareth request that donation, we also arranged for him to tour the school and hand over the cheque to them in person. Fantastic bloke.

Like Gareth, I also took on an additional role involving QPR that season. It came about after Geraldine rang me from Loftus Road, with Gianni wanting to know if I could 'help him out' on matchdays. His main concern was finding someone to take over the role of matchday announcer, introducing the teams onto the pitch and that kind of thing. I wasn't too sure I'd be suited to that – unlike Paul Morrissey, who had only just joined the media department at that time and eventually ended up taking it on a few years down the line. Paul has the ideal voice and manner for that kind of thing and it's testament to his all-round skill set that he's still at the club to this day!

However, one other aspect of matchday activities that did interest me was providing the live in-house commentary. This was the commentary that the club would use for their highlights packages and special features on the website, as well as end-of-season compilations and so on. I was told the commentary was also piped live into hospitality areas during matches, not that I'd expect too many people to be keenly listening out for commentary on a game they could see perfectly well for themselves.

Gianni seemed happy with that idea and so did Jackie Bass, who had taken over from Phil as the head of the media department. It was similar to what I'd done previously on Clubcall and Planet Online – except that, instead of sitting in the press box, this gig involved heading over to the other side of the stadium and ascending to the gantry that hung from the roof of the Ellerslie Road Stand. Frankly, it was quite a thrill getting to walk down the tunnel, then around the touchline past the Loft while the players were warming up. It helped to fuel that heart-warming emotion of being part of the club I loved, the sense of making some kind of contribution to the club while enjoying myself into the bargain. I don't want to exaggerate, making out I was given free rein to go anywhere I chose at Loftus Road, but little things, like being given the passcode to gain access to the offices on the top floor – to collect and return the broadcasting kit – all made me feel more welcome.

And here's something I should make completely clear, I never asked for or received a penny from the club while I was the matchday commentator at that time. I'm not saying that to play the noble martyr, I just want to stress there was no financial incentive. The way I viewed it, this was an opportunity to help out my club, where I still believed everyone was pulling in the same direction. Maybe that sounds overly sentimental and clichéd. But I genuinely felt at the time I was a piece – a very small piece, granted – in the QPR jigsaw and that's why it made me so unhappy to see that jigsaw broken up entirely, to be replaced with a glossy 3D upgrade that turned out to be complete tat.

I realised fairly quickly that it was good practice to make sure you paid a visit to the gents en route to the Ellerslie Road gantry … getting caught short up there really didn't bear thinking about! It was also something of a shock to learn that the gantry swayed with the energy of the crowd in the seats below when they celebrated a QPR goal. I didn't have any fears that the structure was insecure and might pitch me headlong into Row J or anything like that, it was just an alarming sensation the first time I felt it in the first home match of the season. With that said, I was feeling as euphoric as anyone at that moment, having witnessed one of the club's youth-team graduates, Shabazz Baidoo, score in the 90th minute to secure a 2-2 draw against Leeds.

Overall, it wasn't too bad a start to the new season. Nick Ward got his first Rangers goal in a home win against Southend a few days later and the team should have backed that up with another victory away to Preston, only to concede a late equaliser. Still, five points from four games looked solid enough. The main problem was that both of the previous year's first-choice centre-backs, Shittu and Georges Santos, had gone and Zesh Rehman, who had made the short journey from Fulham, wasn't really coming up to scratch as a replacement.

It was hard not to feel sorry for Zesh, a thoroughly nice man who you really wanted to see succeed at Loftus Road, but it just never happened. Later that season the club got involved with a PR drive to promote recycling and poor Zesh was chosen – or maybe volunteered – to take part in the resulting photo opportunity, which involved him donning a pair of Marigolds to sift through a pile of rubbish. Given some of his performances on the field, I'm afraid it was one of those captions that almost wrote itself.

A month or so into the season I took the train down to Plymouth for Rangers' reunion with their former manager. It was evident that Ollie was still seething about Gary Waddock's remarks – which, as I've said, I feel were misinterpreted – but he was also quite candid after the game, which finished in a 1-1 draw, when reflecting on his departure from Loftus Road. For the first time, Ollie was able to be completely open about QPR's recruitment process, saying, 'I was starved of cash to buy anybody and decisions about players to buy weren't mine.'

That point at Home Park would be the last one QPR gained under Waddock's management, as it turned out. The team dropped to the foot of the table after losing at Colchester – my first visit to the Essex club's old Layer Road ground and memorable for the fact that you had to basically clamber over a flat roof backing onto somebody's garden in order to access the commentary position. I can recall one of the home broadcasters observing, after Rangers had pulled a goal back from 2-0 down, that we were in for a 'grandstand finish'. As Tony Incenzo pointed out, it was a pity Colchester didn't actually have a grandstand or anything that resembled one.

Although Gianni had been muttering darkly 'he needs help' as the team's form began to dip, I still hadn't seen Waddock's demotion coming as rapidly as it did. Rumours began to appear in the tabloids that John Gregory, who had been out of the management game since leaving Derby three and a half years earlier, was on his way to Loftus Road, but I can't say I took a great deal of notice. Then, after Rangers had crashed out of the League Cup at Port Vale a few days later, the club sent around an email announcing a press conference the following afternoon.

Naively, I phoned Jackie Bass to ask what it was all about. 'Well, what do you think?' she replied, understandably incredulous that I hadn't cottoned on. I suppose I knew really, but I just hoped it might be something else. I felt sad and disappointed that it hadn't worked out for Gary and, wondering what the next manager would be like to deal with, I made my way over to Loftus Road.

# 4

# AIR OF OPTIMISM IN THE CAMP

## (February 2007)

Perhaps the most curious aspect of the press gathering to announce John Gregory's return to QPR was the presence of Gary Waddock, the man he was replacing in the dugout. The club's official line was that Gary would be staying on as Gregory's assistant, so the former manager sat there to one side, unsurprisingly looking somewhat sheepish while Gianni and Gregory fielded questions. It seemed a very strange set-up. Could you imagine, for instance, a scenario where Tony Blair loitered behind Gordon Brown while he gave his first address as Prime Minister, having agreed to take over at the Foreign Office? Hardly likely. In many ways this should have been viewed as proof of miscalculation on Gianni's part, having trumpeted Gary Waddock's managerial credentials for months and then lost faith in him six weeks into the new season.

The new manager dutifully sat down to meet the regulars, including myself, and answer a few further questions. I asked Gregory to clarify what the managerial shake-up would mean for Alan McDonald who, like Gary, had also been a team-mate when he wore the blue-and-white hoops. Although the initial reply was that he hadn't yet decided on what role, if any, Macca would have, it was no great surprise when his departure was announced later that week.

My initial impressions of Gregory? He came across as a skilled operator, someone who knew the right things to say, highlighting his past association with the club. There were references to a Shepherd's Bush pie 'n' mash shop, praise for the 'ledge' Terry Venables and some hints that his predecessor might learn from Gregory's own early managerial experiences, when he had been sacked by Portsmouth. And he was quite open about his desire to transform the training ground culture at QPR – which, given that he ran his own mobile phone business, seemed slightly surprising.

'I don't want mobile phones going off all the time, people getting off the bus with a headset on,' Gregory announced. 'I don't have ghetto blasters or any of that in the dressing room – you're here to play football and win matches.'

He was certainly consistent about that – at least one younger player later incurred Gregory's displeasure by wearing headphones in the dressing room and found himself frozen out of the first-team picture. There was another remark made by the manager on that first day which, it could be said, went some way towards explaining an infamous event that followed a few months down the line.

'I love to see people that want to punch each other on the training ground. I don't mind players getting into a ruck. If you've not had a fight on the training ground in a month, you've got a problem.'

In the context of that philosophy, Gregory's decision to appoint Richard Hill as his number two made perfect sense!

Hill, whose arrival further muddied the water around Gary Waddock's role and paved the way for the former manager's departure, lasted just four months before he was sacked for his part in what became labelled 'the Great Brawl of China' by one of the tabloids. It was another embarrassing episode for the club, who had just about recovered from the negative PR of the 'gun in the boardroom' court case, and found themselves in the headlines again for all the wrong reasons. With the Olympics in Beijing less than 18 months away, China's Under-23 side – who would be representing their country at the Games – took on Rangers in a training-ground friendly. The game descended into a mass punch-up, with Hill facing a police charge after one of the Chinese players was hospitalised with a broken jaw. Understandably, the Rangers players who had witnessed the ruck weren't allowed to speak publicly about it – but one of them did tell me, off the record, he had little doubt Hill would lose his job.

I never had the chance to speak to Hill during his brief stay at QPR – and I was left wishing I hadn't spoken to the other man who joined Gregory's backroom staff during the early days. Joe Dunbar, who arrived with the fancy title of sports performance manager – certainly not a job description ever seen before at QPR – had worked with some big non-football names, including world heavyweight boxing champion Lennox Lewis and Olympic middle distance star Dame Kelly Holmes. I've no reason to doubt he had a positive effect on the players at Loftus Road, but one thing was made quite clear – he didn't like me.

Later in the season, Dunbar was deputed to speak to the local reporters after one game and, if I remember rightly, Paul Morrissey introduced him to myself and Paul Warburton, who had been covering the game for the *Paddington Mercury*. When he heard my name, Dunbar broke into an icy, unsmiling stare and replied stiffly, 'Yes, I know who you are.'

Well, that's a kind of fame, I suppose – but it certainly didn't sound as though he'd meant that in a positive way. 'Erm, from where?' I inquired tentatively.

'I read what you wrote in the Stoke programme,' Dunbar offered by way of explanation and suddenly his distaste became clearer. The Stoke media department had contacted me a few weeks earlier, asking if I could answer a few questions about how Rangers' season was going for the match programme ahead of their trip to the Britannia Stadium. I'd expressed some disappointment at the way some of the younger first-teamers – including the headphone-wearing player – had found their opportunities restricted under the Gregory regime and suggested little effort had been made to help progress their careers. I could understand his reaction to the criticism – if anything, I was genuinely surprised he'd bothered to read the programme, much less take umbrage! In fairness to Dunbar, having made his view known, he was still willing to answer my questions, albeit without much enthusiasm. Warbo seemed to think the whole thing was hilarious, telling me he'd rarely seen anyone given as filthy a look as the one Dunbar had sent in my direction!

By that time, everyone had long grown used to the manager's unpredictability when it came to post-match media duties. Gregory's tendency to give the whole thing a swerve if he didn't fancy it first became apparent just two games after his arrival – both of which had resulted in Rangers victories, against Hull and Southampton. So you might have assumed he'd be happy to talk up the new manager bounce a little. However, a lengthy wait outside the away dressing room at St Mary's failed to bear fruit, and Ian Taylor, the press officer on duty that day, emerged with an air of bewilderment and embarrassment to convey the message that Gregory wouldn't be taking part in any interviews. No further explanation! I remember walking back to the station with Tony Incenzo, who was just as bemused as I was, as we speculated on the possible reasons for Gregory's no-show. Before too long, it became evident that there was only one reason – he was someone who liked being in control and reminding everyone of that by indulging in little games.

It was a similar situation a few weeks later after Rangers' match against Luton at Kenilworth Road – from which, incidentally, the visitors had again picked up three points! However, it was utterly impossible to second-guess Gregory on this kind of thing. Some managers refuse to give post-match interviews after a particularly bad defeat, or a controversial refereeing decision that could, they are shrewd enough to realise, land them in trouble with the FA. With Gregory there was no pattern – it came down purely to his whims or, in the case of that Luton game, he didn't want to stick around because he'd arranged to go and see his musical hero Bruce Springsteen in concert that evening.

Without a doubt, the best illustration of Gregory's bizarre behaviour came after a midweek home game against Sunderland at the end of November, which ended in a 2-1 defeat. Not surprisingly, Sunderland manager Roy Keane was in and out of the press room fairly swiftly after the game – presumably, they would have been heading back to Wearside straight away. It's probably fair to say that just about everyone else was as keen as Keane, so to speak, to wrap up proceedings and begin making their way home. The assembled media, who had either written copy or audio material to file, the three old boys – Ron, Peter and Tony – who looked after the press room on matchdays, and the stadium staff who wanted to lock up. Nobody particularly wanted to hang around Loftus Road until the witching hour, but the wait for Gregory to appear went on and on.

At around 11pm – more than an hour after the game had finished – the club's commercial manager, Gary Hooper, made his way through the door to announce, 'Erm, gentlemen, I'm sorry but the manager won't be coming up tonight. He's, uh, got a bit of a headache.'

Hooper looked uncomfortable enough as he spoke, but it wouldn't have been a surprise if his nose had grown longer at the same time. It was one of the least convincing excuses I've ever heard anyone offer to explain anything. And why on earth was it Hooper's job to cover for the manager? Nobody believed it for one moment and there were a few irate responses hurled in Hooper's direction before he was made to look even more foolish by the door opening once more to reveal … Gregory. Immaculate as always, hair slicked and gleaming as he made his way to his usual seat, with his 'headache' miraculously cured, and opened with a casual, 'Sorry to keep you waiting, gents.'

The manager then proceeded to field questions, eventually finishing with the memorable line, 'Have a good evening.' An odd thing to say considering there were only about 40 minutes left until midnight.

I discovered Gregory could be just as hard to pin down if you wanted to speak to him away from the hurly-burly of matchdays. Don't get me wrong, he was more than happy to hand out his phone number – but far less willing to actually answer or return calls. So I asked him if it'd be possible to have a quick chat in person if I came down to the training ground once a week, much as I'd done with Glenn Roeder and Alan Pardew at West Ham.

'Well, I like to get in early,' Gregory informed me. 'So be there at 8.30 and I can talk to you then.'

I've always tended to be more of an owl than a lark – someone who finds it easier to work late in the evening than early in the morning – and I never choose to drive in heavy traffic if I can avoid it, simply because I'm not a terribly patient driver and get easily stressed in those situations. So getting down to Harlington in rush hour was far from ideal but, if that's what it took to speak to the manager of Queens Park Rangers, then I'd make myself do it.

Fortunately I left myself sufficient time and bowled into the car park at around 8.20 before reporting to Paul Morrissey, who was based at the training ground – and could usually be relied on to sort out a cup of coffee while I awaited the manager.

Paul showed me to the canteen and also obliged on the coffee front as I sat down to wait … and wait. I could probably have made serious inroads on an entire jar of Gold Blend by the time Gregory showed up, at around 9.45. But what I learned was that if you could be bothered to put up with the manager's penchant for making you hang around it was well worth your while. When you finally got to speak to him, he was both interesting and forthcoming, and I gained plenty of stories from those conversations. He had plenty to say, whether on or off the record, about the players he was pleased with, the ones he wasn't and why. In many ways, John Gregory was an old-school type of football manager and I think I can honestly say I enjoyed a better relationship with him than any of the other regulars at around that time did. That might not be saying a great deal! But, incredibly, there would be times a few years down the line when I'd think wistfully about how much easier things had been in the Gregory era.

It did concern me somewhat when he made a point of praising Chelsea and their manager, Jose Mourinho. The manager had tapped into a very useful resource just down the road – Chelsea had a burgeoning stock of young players, the vast majority of them with no chance whatsoever of seeing first-team action at Stamford Bridge. So he enlisted the services of two of the Chelsea youngsters, Jimmy Smith and Michael Mancienne, on loan deals that would eventually be extended for most of that season. Both players performed well at Loftus Road – Smith was a box-to-box midfielder who got his fair share of goals, while Mancienne looked classy on the ball and could play across the defence. However, while Gregory's decision to sign them was a wise one, I felt it was unwise to keep talking up how grateful he was to Chelsea and Mourinho – that wasn't a subject that was likely to go down well among the QPR fanbase. It was strange that Gregory, having played for Rangers in an era when the two west London clubs had been genuine rivals, didn't seem to grasp that.

Interviewing the two lads – Smith more so than Mancienne – also provided an insight into the way young players at Premier League level were now being conditioned to handle media relations. Until speaking to Smith, I'd never seen a player fish out his own phone and start recording before he began to answer your questions! The responses were highly guarded, as well – one of those interviews which last for a reasonable length of time but, when you play it back, it dawns on you that the person you were speaking to has actually said very little of substance. Sometimes they might repeat your own words, sometimes repeating their own and sometimes answering a completely different question to the one that was asked. It's a skill politicians have long since mastered, but this was when it first became clear to me that young footballers were being trained in a similar manner.

That Smith interview came after he'd scored his first QPR goal, in a lively 3-3 draw at home to Norwich – certainly one of those games in which I could feel the Ellerslie Road gantry swaying now and then! I remember I was allowed to take a work experience student up there for the Norwich game, the nephew of a family friend who were all QPR fans, so it probably wasn't a bad match to choose. He emailed me later to say thank you and added the remark, 'What an amazing job you have!' I couldn't have agreed more, it really did feel that way. I absolutely loved doing the commentary, especially for that kind of dramatic, see-saw match, and there was another of those a few weeks later, with Smith scoring twice this time in a 4-2 win over Crystal Palace.

Unfortunately, any thoughts that Rangers might pull clear of the danger zone were dispelled by a run of five straight defeats in the run-up to Christmas, so it was nice to have a bit of a distraction when my friend Brian Melzack invited me to a charity match he was organising. Brian, a lifelong Rangers fan and often unofficial adviser to the club, had been working with an organisation called Saving Faces to help fund research into facial injuries and surgery, and had arranged for a celebrity XI to play against an Army team in Aldershot. Needless to say, Brian's line-up included a number of ex-QPR players, so it was a good opportunity for me to go along and interview a few of them. Karl Ready was refreshingly honest about his Rangers career and so was Andy Sinton, who has since taken on an ambassadorial role with the club and does it exceedingly well. It was particularly interesting to hear Andy discuss the circumstances of his departure from QPR in 1993 because, as a fan, I'd always noticed that he was singled out for booing when he returned to Loftus Road as a Sheffield Wednesday or Spurs player. By contrast, contemporaries such as Les Ferdinand and Paul Parker had been warmly welcomed when they came back in a Newcastle or Manchester United shirt.

'There was a myth that I'd asked to leave,' Sinton told me. 'I didn't. I was very happy at QPR and had no reason to leave. One or two people within the club had a certain amount of power and spun it a particular way, saying I'd wanted to go. Sometimes people believe what they're fed.'

It was a valuable insight – and, further along the line, a valuable warning as to the way spin and PR could be employed to distort the truth at a football club.

I certainly couldn't pass up the opportunity to speak to Dennis Bailey, the hero of the New Year's Day massacre of Manchester United. Dennis spoke fondly about his time at QPR and it made a nice feature, particularly as the 15th anniversary of his Old Trafford hat-trick was only weeks away. In fact, Ian Taylor was keen to run it in the match programme for the New Year's Day game against Colchester and I was more than happy for my work to be reprinted – it helped Ian out during what's always a difficult period with print deadlines and widened my audience beyond the readership of the newspaper and its website. Works for everyone!

The gradual development of newspaper websites, however, was now making it far easier for people to replicate content and pass it off as their own, without any agreement in place or acknowledgement of the original source. I was none too pleased around that time when a rival paper, one of the Newsquest titles, lifted a piece I'd written with quotes from Gianni, stating he'd demand a £10m fee from any club who wanted to sign Lee Cook. In the event, of course, Cookie eventually went to Fulham for far less than that the following summer! But that wasn't the point. Unless they'd been bugging the telephone conversation – and, yes, that kind of thing did go on, but I doubted Gianni was considered high-profile enough to be a victim of phone hacking – there was no way they could have obtained those identical quotes.

In the end, there wasn't a lot I could do other than get my editor to complain to the other editor – and he just came back with some kind of standard reply, suggesting he didn't feel there had been any untoward practice. In all fairness, it was entirely possible that another site had lifted the story in the first place and his paper had picked it up from there. We'd see this kind of thing happening more and more, sometimes even going full circle as one outlet launched the original story and then, after the quotes had passed through about three or four other websites, ran it again – maybe not even recognising where it had come from in the first place.

Sadly, this practice was nothing new – I'd encountered something similar in my *Recorder* days, when a tabloid reporter who lived within the circulation area used to scan the sports pages for quotes he could repackage and flog on a regular basis. At least back then, he had to go and buy a paper instead of a quick copy and paste job off the internet!

I can't say I was all that enamoured at unwittingly doing other people's work for them, but one media outlet I did enjoy contributing to was BBC Radio London. I'd got to know some of their broadcast journalists at matches or training grounds, particularly Phil Parry, who was not only a fellow QPR fan but also an absolute natural behind the microphone. Phil always drove to away matches, whether he was covering Rangers or another London team, and was pretty generous when it came to spare seats. One space in the car would usually be taken up by whichever ex-player was acting as co-commentator – Clive Walker was a regular passenger – but there were often a couple of spaces for regulars such as myself, Noam Friedlander or Yann Tear, who reported for the *Ealing Gazette*. Anyway, I was pleased to be invited onto BBC London's evening sports show as a QPR 'expert' voice a couple of times that season – it was good publicity both for the newspaper and for me personally. To be honest, this kind of thing probably benefits the individual more in terms of helping to establish their credentials among listeners. Generally, fellow Rangers supporters were a lot more likely to recognise my name than to know which publications I worked for, and I'd be surprised if that wasn't the same for most journalists, especially since the growth of Twitter and other forms of social media.

With that said, at least John Gregory did know who I wrote for. That became clear at QPR's AGM that season – an unusually lively gathering that featured a heated exchange between Gianni and Harold Winton, the club president. I don't actually recall why I attended – I'd never been to an AGM before, even when I was a shareholder back in the Chris Wright era – but Gregory noticed and I duly received a namecheck. Well, a namecheck of sorts. I've been called many things in my life, but Gregory remains the only person to address me as 'Benjy' on a regular basis. He'd been asked to do a question-and-answer session with some of the shareholders and mostly played it for laughs. A female member of the audience asked the manager whether he'd be trying to sign Lee Camp on a permanent basis, to which Gregory's initial response was, 'Why? Do you fancy him?'

Having given a more serious answer about the prospects of a deal for Camp, the manager concluded, 'And that's off the record. I don't want to read it in the *Kilburn Times* next week, Benjy.' Not much I could do other than smile and shake my head to assure him I'd find some other means of filling column inches. Joking aside, that's how it ought to be if you value the manager's trust and aim to retain it.

Going back to BBC London, I made my debut on a show presented by Steve Bunce, best known as a boxing man but perfectly capable of holding a lively discussion about many other subjects. I felt it went well, even right at the end of the conversation when he put me on the spot, asking me to predict whether Rangers would avoid relegation or not. 'Of course they will,' I replied cheerfully, trying to portray a confidence I didn't really have at that moment. In reality, the team's prospects of Championship survival were looking none too good, especially after a 5-0 walloping by Southend which came just a few days after the training ground bust-up with the Chinese team. It proved to be the end of the road for Simon Royce, who copped much of the blame from Gregory after shipping five goals against his former club and was immediately dropped from the team.

In a strange way, though, that Roots Hall horror show was probably the turning point for Rangers. More than one player later told me how the raucous Southend celebrations that night had helped to spur them on for the rest of the season – and, come May, it was the Essex side who sank into League One.

It wasn't until the victory at Leicester in March that I genuinely thought the team might be capable of staying up. The trip to the Walkers Stadium was one I shared with Phil and Clive, who were both of a similar opinion as we moved along the northbound carriageway of the M1 – but second thoughts began to creep in after we'd witnessed an unexpected 3-1 away win, including an equally unexpected 25-yard sizzler from the right boot of Marc Nygaard.

I reckoned Rangers still needed to win four of their remaining eight games to do it – and, in fact, they took only six to reach that target. The atmosphere at Loftus Road for wins against Preston, Luton and Cardiff was magnificent – it felt as if, somehow, the fighting spirit of the promotion season in 2004 had suddenly been rediscovered at the back of a cupboard. The abiding image of the Cardiff game, when survival was confirmed, was Marcus Bignot – who began the season on the transfer list and ended it with the captain's armband – grabbing a microphone and belting out 'We are the Rangers boys' to the celebrating crowd.

For once, QPR had succeeded in getting their transfer policy right during the second half of that season. Adam Bolder, who had previously played under Gregory at Derby, brought better organisation in the middle of the park, and Danny Cullip added the physical presence in defence that had been missing since the sale of Shittu. Camp, returning for a second loan spell, was a popular choice to replace Royce in goal and yet another ex-Derby man, Inigo Idiakez, also played his part during a brief loan at Loftus Road. It seemed fairly clear that, by and large, these had been the manager's choice rather than the chairman's. Even Gianni had apparently begun to acknowledge the flaws in a recruitment system that had landed QPR with the likes of Armel, Adam Czerkas, Ugo Ukah and countless others of limited ability. He told me, 'I think we have to be more careful in terms of looking at a player a little longer and deciding whether he can fit into our system. But the bottom line is that the manager decides.'

The mood after that Cardiff game was euphoric and yet … there were ominous signs that many of the people who had seemed to be part of the furniture at QPR were being swept away. Kevin Gallen had already reunited with Ollie at Plymouth after falling from favour under Gregory, while Matthew Rose had also left the club and Paul Furlong and Birch were among the players to be released when their contracts came to an end. Birch bowed out in typically belligerent fashion, observing that he'd helped to upset Stoke one final time – the Potters' 1-1 draw at Loftus Road on the last day of the season ended their hopes of reaching the play-offs. But he also confidently – and accurately – declared, 'In the long run I will be back, whether it's as a player or coach. The reason I played football was to play for QPR and I fulfilled my dream.'

Cook, who had looked outstanding at times that season, would be sold that summer, with Bignot departing six months later. The promotion-winning squad had been well and truly broken up, the winds of change were in motion. However, you'd need to have been blessed with truly prophetic insight to imagine just how sweeping those winds would be.

# 5

# COOK MOVE PREVENTS CASH CRISIS

## (July 2007)

The summer break can be a strange time when you're reporting on a football club. If you're a cricket fan like myself, it offers you the chance to spend more time watching (and writing about) a different subject for a while. It doesn't have to be cricket, obviously – there are plenty of other sports that command attention during the summer months, such as the grass court season in tennis, rugby league and various athletics tournaments, in addition to the Olympics once every four years. At the same time, though, you do need to keep your coverage of the football club ticking over, even if it might be just one story in each edition – and, with no actual matches taking place, some thinking outside the box becomes essential. In previous summers, I'd been able to contact the QPR manager over the phone for updates now and then – but, although I'd established a good working relationship with Gregory, his habit of ignoring calls and messages hadn't changed.

Initially, there were still opportunities to speak to players with QPR connections who hadn't yet finished the season. The opening of the new, revamped Wembley Stadium in the spring of 2007 was ideal for a newspaper rooted in the borough of Brent, with the regeneration of the area around the stadium giving us a boost in terms of both editorial and advertising. It also made it easier for us to gain media accreditation for matches at the stadium, so I made my way down there for the FA Trophy Final between Stevenage and Kidderminster. It turned out to be a classic final, with Stevenage coming from 2-0 down to win – rather like a certain other team had done in 1967 – and I was able to grab a word with ex-

Rangers midfielder Adam Miller afterwards. Fortunately, Miller remembered me from his 18-month stint at Loftus Road and was happy to wax lyrical about the joy of winning at Wembley and how he'd love to come and watch QPR do the same in the future. Hopefully he made it down there in 2014!

I was back at the national stadium a week later to witness its first FA Cup Final, which I can't honestly say I enjoyed. The game itself, between Manchester United and Chelsea, was terrible to watch – nowhere near as entertaining as the show Miller and his Stevenage team-mates had put on the previous weekend. Secondly, a Didier Drogba goal in extra time ensured that Chelsea lifted the trophy – not a sentence I'd ever choose to either type or read.

Not long afterwards came news of another one-time Chelsea centre-forward, Mick Harford – who was joining Rangers as Gregory's new assistant. Warren Neill had been helping out at the end of the previous season on a temporary basis following Richard Hill's downfall, but Harford's credentials, having just assisted Colchester to a top-ten Championship finish, made him a strong candidate.

With this kind of news, it's easy enough to bring up the club website, note down the details and accompanying quotes from the person in question and repackage those into a story for your paper. Sometimes there's no more you can do than that. But, personally, I always tried to think about how I could provide something different, moving on from the initial story to offer the readers a new angle or information they might find interesting. Why would they pick up a newspaper to read exactly the same thing they'd already seen on the QPR home page?

Instead, I reasoned, you should use the internet for another reason – to check, in this case, where and when Mick Harford had coached previously, then to flick through your contacts book, see who might have worked with him and could potentially offer an interesting – and unique – perspective. As most of those who have worked with me will know, I'm not a great fan of tagging stories 'exclusive' unless they really, really merit it! I feel it should be taken as read, more often than not, that the interview you're preparing to cast your eye over is one you cannot see anywhere else. It became something of a running joke a few years later when QPR, by then a club rapidly disappearing up its own backside, repeatedly tagged items on their website as 'exclusive'. Was that meant to impress people, I wondered? Maybe we should have offered congratulations on the laudable achievement of obtaining quotes from your boss or work colleague.

In this instance, the name that stood out for me was that of Jamie Cureton – a former QPR striker and one who had banged in 28 goals for Colchester the previous season. I rang Jamie and he readily obliged, telling me how Harford would give him tips on opposing defenders just before kick-off and giving him a great deal of credit for the team's overachievement. He also predicted that some of the squad might follow Harford to Loftus Road and, as it turned out, Chris Barker and Hogan Ephraim, who had both been on loan at Colchester, did rock up at QPR before the start of the new season.

Inevitably, Gianni continued to be my main source of information during the close season as Rangers brought in new players – most of whom, it should be said, looked far more sensible additions to the squad than had been the case the previous summer. But the main topic of discussion – and concern – over the summer was undoubtedly the club's financial position. The £10m loan by Panamanian-based company ABC, which had enabled Rangers to come out of administration back in 2002, was now weighing the club down significantly and Gianni was openly becoming desperate for help.

'Time is very short,' he admitted. 'The rate of interest is going up and we need somebody with a lot of money who can buy off the ABC loan. The door is open and this is the time, if there's anybody out there with QPR at heart, to come in. We need people who are serious, not a waste of time.'

I can't say I've ever found financial issues particularly interesting, but this was one that demanded some attention. I became a persistent caller – maybe bordering on nuisance caller, even – to the Football League's communications department as it became apparent that Rangers had accepted money from the Oldham Athletic chairman to help refinance the ABC loan. Unsurprisingly, speculation followed in one or two national newspapers that the League board would investigate the matter, with phrases such as 'points deduction' being bandied around, although in the end they appeared to be satisfied that the money had been repaid.

Sadly, this seemed fairly typical of the way that, if QPR made headlines in the national press, it tended to be for all the wrong reasons – as evidenced by the Great Brawl of China earlier that year. In my view, this was precisely why the club and the local papers should maintain a close relationship – more often than not, we tried to take a more holistic approach and give coverage to what Rangers were doing well, along with what they did badly. Nevertheless, you could sense the storm clouds gathering as pre-season approached, with barrister Nick de Marco – who had joined the board – confirming to me that the eventual sale of Lee Cook to Fulham had, in effect, kept the threat of administration at bay for the time being.

Cook's move had long been inevitable, but another exit at around the same time – that of youth-team boss Joe Gallen – was cause for concern, particularly without any explanation given and the fact that it had quickly followed his brother Kevin's departure. Joe had done a good job with the youngsters and, whether or not his surname had counted against him, it was another indication that the club might no longer be setting such stall by the youth policy it had once favoured. Fortunately Joe linked up again with Kenny Jackett, who had been Ollie's assistant during the promotion campaign, and the pair went on to help Millwall back into the Championship a few years later.

Rangers' pre-season programme, at least, was a fairly attractive one – with Celtic packing out Loftus Road for a prestigious friendly and Fulham, with Cook lining up for his new team, also making the short journey to the Bush. The latter game turned out to be something of a false dawn, with Ben Sahar – who had signed on loan from Chelsea, along with the returning Michael Mancienne – scoring both goals in Rangers' 2-1 win. Sadly, the sight of Sahar hitting the net was not one QPR fans would witness again. There was also a less pleasant spectacle for the Loftus Road crowd that night, with another of the recent arrivals, midfielder Simon Walton, stretchered off after breaking his leg.

I was sorry for Walton, who had arrived with a promising reputation after spells at Leeds and Charlton and was now facing the prospect of months out injured before his QPR career had even got going. There was also a practical consideration for me to wrestle with, having interviewed Walton a couple of days before his injury with the intention of printing it in our next edition!

All you can really do, in those circumstances, is review the player's comments and judge whether it's possible to salvage the feature in the light of more recent events. Sometimes there's no alternative but to bin it entirely, but I think that should be a last resort. In this case, Walton had spoken about turning down other Championship offers to sign for QPR and I felt that was a strong enough angle on which to rehash the interview. I couldn't help but make comparison with Richard Ord, who had signed for Rangers some years earlier, but was injured in a pre-season friendly and never played for the club, or any other club, again. Walton did at least make a comeback that winter but, with the landscape dramatically altered by then, his chances of playing a significant role at QPR were gone.

That week, leading up to the start of the season, also presented me with a potentially more serious headache, an affliction known as Football DataCo. For as long as I could remember – and far longer than that, presumably – the process of securing a seat in the press box at a football ground had been fairly straightforward. It involved sending a fax or, more recently, an email – although some clubs continued to insist on faxes – to the relevant member of staff at the club in question, who would authorise a pass in your name. Occasionally there might be a glitch if demand was high for a particular match and you could end up in an 'overflow' seat outside the actual press box, but by and large the process worked.

However, the Premier League and Football League brought in stricter guidelines to control media coverage, to be overseen – policed might be more accurate – by a company named Football DataCo. Even information such as fixture lists and stats were suddenly classified as 'intellectual property' and limits were placed on the frequency of live reports from matches – with every media outlet now required to apply for a DataCo licence each year. And unless that licence was granted, you wouldn't officially be allowed to report on any games.

So, what did you need to apply for the all-important licence? Three things. To complete and sign a lengthy legal agreement, to provide proof of your organisation's public liability insurance – in our case, a document pinned to the wall above the photocopier – and to send relevant cuttings from the previous season. Half a dozen cuttings, maybe? Oh no. Thirty was the required minimum number, which meant a laborious process of thumbing through last year's back copies and hoping the printer wouldn't jam under the strain. Which, with three or four of us all dealing with this procedure at the same time, often proved a forlorn hope.

In a way, none of this was a bad thing because, until then, it had been all too easy for people to abuse the system. By dint of knowing the right individuals, it wasn't too hard for chancers with no journalistic credentials whatsoever to treat themselves regularly to an afternoon of free football and refreshments, while claiming to work for an obscure publication or radio station. There was one character on the circuit who professed to report on games for an expat newspaper in Australia – and, with the internet still in its infancy, it was difficult for anyone to confidently call his bluff!

The flaw in the DataCo procedure was that it placed all power in the hands of one man. An extremely unhelpful man named Derek Johnston, who I later learned had started out with responsibility for handing out the bibs to photographers at Anfield and collecting them after the game. Somehow he'd worked his way up to the top of the DataCo pole and now wielded supreme authority over issuing or withholding licences. That was the problem confronting me, when we got to the Monday before QPR's opening game away to Bristol City, and the newspaper's licence still hadn't arrived.

The rest of the staff at DataCo HQ were as helpful and sympathetic as they could be, but it was made clear that I would need to contact Derek – who happened to be away all week. As you would be in the days leading up to the start of a new football season.

Eventually I got through to the great man on his mobile and explained that I'd posted all the required documents to him a few weeks earlier but had yet to receive confirmation of the licence. 'Well, I haven't seen them,' came the reply. 'You'll have to send them again.'

Yes, of course I could do that – but would they be able to issue the licence number in time to validate my attendance at Ashton Gate? 'Sorry, I can't help you. I'm not back until next week so you won't be able to go,' was Mr Johnston's response, hinting from his tone that he'd prefer to concentrate on his sunlounger rather than facilitate my trip to Bristol. And, yes, only he could authorise the licence, there'd be no point in my nagging at his underlings to help me out.

Fortunately, Bristol City's press officer turned out to be a far more relaxed and reasonable individual when I rang him and explained the problem. 'I'm not bothered about all that,' he told me. 'Just send me a fax on headed paper, that'll do. See you at the game!'

But for his commendable flexibility, I'd have had to miss seeing Rangers come from behind twice to draw 2-2, with Damion Stewart heading a last-minute equaliser. As well as the fact that I obviously enjoyed being there, it was also important in that, with the newspaper now moving to a publication date of Thursday instead of Wednesday, it became easier to devote more space to the game. That didn't only mean me writing more words, it was more about putting together a decent picture spread with a crop of images from Dave Brennan, a fellow QPR fan I knew through his involvement with a local Sunday league and also a very capable photographer. Dave and I ended up travelling to a number of away games together over the next few years, and it's always a pleasant surprise when I bump into him at a football ground nowadays.

The delightful Mr Johnston did grudgingly approve our DataCo licence once he returned to base, not that it mattered to Ian Taylor, who was by then in charge of the QPR media department and had already added my name to the list for the midweek League Cup tie against Leyton Orient. In any case, I was still doing the club commentary so I'd have been surprised if he declined to let me in without proof of a licence! To nobody's great surprise, Rangers were knocked out of a cup competition by lower league opposition at the first hurdle. By then, it had become such a predictable outcome – with no disrespect to Orient intended – that any references to a 'cup shock' had ceased to seem appropriate.

I decided it was about time to write a story highlighting Rangers' appalling cup record and rang the club's long-serving secretary Sheila Marson to find out whether it was in fact compulsory for QPR to enter cup competitions. It was only partly tongue in cheek – I didn't know the answer – but Sheila chuckled when I reminded her that one of her predecessors had actually forgotten to submit an application to enter the FA Cup during the 1920s and suggested it might not be too disastrous if it slipped her mind as well! Not that I could ever have imagined that happening – Sheila was known to be highly efficient in her role and the club's decision to ditch her a couple of years later made little sense.

Meanwhile, one of the names whose involvement would come to symbolise bad decision-making at QPR in the future was beginning to appear on the radar. I wasn't a fan of Formula One to any degree, so I knew little about Flavio Briatore, other than that he was a wealthy man and apparently willing to invest in the club. But his proposed takeover seemed to have driven a wedge between Gianni and Antonio Caliendo, with the latter issuing a baffling statement to say the club was not for sale – totally contradicting what the chairman had been saying all summer.

What I did know, however, was that Briatore's bid for QPR was not the only option on the table. Stephen Perry, whose son Jack had been on the club's books a couple of years earlier, had also met with Gianni and, as I understood it, agreed to invest the funds required to wipe out the ABC loan and purchase Caliendo's shares. For whatever reasons, that deal failed to clear the final hurdle – but it's important to make the point that the 'Briatore or bust' line subsequently spun by people at the club was a myth.

However, hand on heart, I really didn't have an opinion at the time on whether Briatore's projected arrival would be good news or bad. Like most Rangers fans, I was more concerned about what was happening on the pitch, with the Orient defeat followed by another insipid performance at home to Cardiff. It was hard to escape the conclusion that the uncertainty over the club's future might be getting to the players, but there should be no great cause for panic after just three games. Next up was a trip to Burnley and, while Rangers' recent record at Turf Moor didn't inspire much optimism, I felt there was a fair chance the team wouldn't come back empty-handed.

Nobody could possibly have imagined the dreadful reason that the team would come back from Burnley without even kicking a ball.

# 6

# MOURNING A STAR

## (August 2007)

August 25 2007.

I was in the passenger seat of Phil Parry's car, heading north towards Turf Moor, and so far the traffic had been favourable as we turned on to the M6. Suddenly my phone rang.

Paul Morrissey wanted to know if I was on my way to the game. Yes, I replied, wondering if he'd rung to warn us of congestion further up the motorway.

'Ben, just to let you know, the game is off,' Paul said. 'Are you with Phil? You might as well turn around and head home.'

I was taken aback and, as would most people in response to what seemed like fairly bizarre advice, I wanted to know more.

'I can't tell you now, but you'll find out soon enough,' Paul replied cryptically. 'Just take it from me, the game is off. Wanted to save you both a wasted journey.'

Having relayed this information to Phil, he agreed we should pull in at the nearest motorway services – if I remember rightly, somewhere near Birmingham, and make some phone calls to try and find out what had happened. But we both knew there could only be a very serious reason for the match to be called off at such short notice.

I called Gareth Ainsworth, who was out injured at the time and hadn't travelled to Burnley, but it was possible he might have been in touch with someone in the squad and would have some idea of what was going on. Gareth hadn't, but he was puzzled and concerned and said he'd try ringing some of his team-mates to find out the reason for the postponement.

When I rejoined Phil, his calls had yielded more information. He broke the news to me that 18-year-old Rangers striker Ray Jones had been killed in a car crash in the early hours of that morning.

That kind of news always comes as a shock and is difficult to process, as I'm quite sure it was for every QPR supporter when they made that grim discovery. It didn't only apply to QPR supporters that day – during the drive back to London I remember receiving text messages from friends and colleagues, people who were football fans, utterly horrified at the loss of a young life in such circumstances.

I'd interviewed Ray Jones a few times in the year since he'd scored his first senior goal for the club, against Northampton. He came across so well as a likeable, modest young man without a hint of the cockiness that some teenagers tend to exhibit, whether footballers or otherwise. There was no doubt as to his potential – he'd already represented England at under-19 level and Premier League sides had been sniffing around him, with Gianni quick to voice outrage at what he viewed as a paltry offer from Fulham earlier that year.

The atmosphere in the car was fairly muted as Phil drove us back to London and it occurred to me that we should make our way towards Loftus Road. Fans who hadn't been travelling to Burnley might well have been to the ground to pay their respects already, and I realised I would need to start thinking about how best to cover this tragic event in the paper.

The rail outside the main entrance was already strewn with QPR scarves and pennants, as well as a row of bouquets and a poster of Ray in action. I'm sure there are some journalists who are much harder-nosed than me and don't mind conducting an impromptu vox pop in response to someone's unexpected passing. For me, it was never an aspect of the job I felt comfortable with and I'd hoped it was something I'd left behind in my early days as a news reporter. But, despite my reluctance, I knew I needed to go and encourage some of the fans to share their reactions to the news and their memories of watching Ray play. In many ways, it was like listening to others articulate my own feelings of sadness and disbelief – and also the sense of loss that was even more keenly felt because Ray was a player who had come through from our youth team. It was still a time when that mattered to QPR fans – we'd felt such pride at the emergence of Alan McDonald, of Kevin Gallen, of Richard Langley because they were homegrown players and we all craved more. Nobody will ever know for certain, but it's possible that Ray Jones might have gone on to enter his name into that pantheon too.

Some of those I spoke to that afternoon also referenced Kiyan Prince, the 15-year-old youth-team player who had been stabbed to death outside his school months earlier. That horrific news had also prompted shock and grief among Rangers fans – not that the vast majority of them would ever have seen Kiyan play football, or even been aware of his existence. Their reactions stemmed from an instinctive kinship towards the wider 'QPR family' and the pain was magnified, I'm sure, for those who had met Ray Jones and asked him for his autograph, watched him play and score goals for the first team. And once again, the proximity of these two tragedies served to underline the regularity with which bad news seemed to surround our club. I remember hearing the word 'cursed' bandied around more than once. All things considered, QPR felt like a club desperate to experience better times, which may be one of the reasons that the straw offered by Flavio Briatore would be grasped so eagerly.

Returning to my desk on Monday, I had to liaise with the news desk, who were running the story of Ray's death on the front page. Because he'd grown up in East Ham and the accident had taken place there, my former *Recorder* colleagues were also covering the story and that meant I needed to concentrate on a different tack in the sports section. As well as running the fans' tributes, I tried to speak to those who had worked closely with Ray at QPR and could outline his qualities as a person as much as a footballer.

Although I didn't have a contact number for John O'Brien, the youth development officer who had first spotted Ray Jones playing Sunday League football, I was able to get hold of Joe Gallen and Gary Waddock. Both spoke about him in glowing terms, with Joe describing him as 'the best prospect we'd had at this club since Nigel Quashie'. Joe had accompanied Ray's mother, Lorraine, to see his England under-19 debut at Walsall the previous season, and predicted that he would have gone on to become a full international. Gary, who was now managing Aldershot Town, recalled how Ray had thanked him after appearing in Rangers' senior side for the first time and helped us to paint a lovely picture of a genuine, down-to-earth boy who was keen to keep learning and improving. I was grateful for what Joe and Gary had to say, not just because of the tributes themselves but because they tied in with my own impressions of Ray on the occasions I'd met him.

Gareth, of course, dedicated his weekly column to Ray Jones's memory and added some nice anecdotes as well, marvelling at his tendency to fall asleep at the drop of a hat on the team bus, in a hospital waiting room or anywhere else. He also mentioned a recent incident when he and Ray did a swimming session as part of their rehab – but while Gareth found himself working hard to tread water in the deep end, the point of the exercise was somewhat lost on the younger man, being tall enough to touch the bottom of the pool!

Overall, I hope we did justice to Ray Jones in that edition and, inevitably, the atmosphere at Loftus Road was emotional when the team returned to action against Southampton that weekend, with every Rangers player sporting a shirt with Ray's name on the back. Despite all the pre-match talk of being motivated to gain their first win of the season in Ray's memory, the team were utterly outclassed in a 3-0 defeat. I must admit, that surprised me – usually, in those situations, the opposition tend to be little more than cannon fodder for a side fired up by recent tragedy. I remembered thinking how Nottingham Forest, for instance, must have felt they were in a no-win situation when they faced Liverpool in the rescheduled FA Cup semi-final following the Hillsborough disaster. As recent events had proved, there were far more important things than a poor start to the Championship season – but you couldn't help thinking the prospective new owners must be unimpressed by three home defeats in a row.

After the Southampton match, I was surprised – and extremely honoured – to be asked by Paul Morrissey if I'd say a few words at the service of remembrance for Ray, to be held at St Stephen & St Thomas Church, just around the corner from Loftus Road, later that week. His family had requested a private funeral, so the service – led by the QPR chaplain Bob Mayo – was an alternative way for the club and supporters to pay their respects. I was touched that Phil Parry and I were the only members of the media invited to contribute – largely, I guess, because we were both QPR fans – but it highlighted the way the club, at that time, valued those links with the local media and included us as part of their community, a community in mourning.

I'd promised Gary Waddock I would let him know the details of a memorial service for Ray, so I rang him back again and he duly turned up at the church, along with another ex-QPR manager in Gerry Francis. I remember Paul Furlong was among the former players who sent a wreath to the service and Mark Barry, the club's sports scientist, gave a personal tribute to Ray. Phil read out some of the condolence messages sent to the club by the big names of the game, such as Alex Ferguson, and then it was my turn.

I can't deny I felt rather nervous about addressing the congregation – at that time, I'd never previously spoken at a memorial service or anything similar. However, in a way it wasn't all that different to speaking on BBC London – albeit formally and with a far more serious tone. This was the brief tribute I delivered:

*'From talking to those who worked with Ray and knew him well, it confirmed the impression I'd formed from the three or four times I'd interviewed him.*

*Ray always came across as a friendly, intelligent young man, very relaxed and laid-back. He was modest, almost to the point of being humble, and seemed genuinely proud to be a professional footballer for QPR.*

*The last time I spoke to Ray was during pre-season and I asked him how he felt last season had gone – a season that he began, let's not forget, as a second-year scholar.*

*His response was, "Well, it went all right, but I can do a lot more." I think everyone here knows that Ray Jones was much better than just "all right".*

*He would certainly have gone on to do a lot more and maybe become a QPR legend, but what he'd achieved already in such a short time won't be forgotten.'*

Looking back at this dreadful tragedy years later, I now feel it was highly symbolic for the club. At the risk of sounding flippant, it wasn't only Ray Jones the human being who was laid to rest at that time. It was also the process Ray had represented at QPR – unearthing and nurturing a talented young footballer, sharpening his ability and introducing him to the first team. In the decade that followed Ray's untimely death, the club essentially lost interest in trying to replicate what he had achieved. One way in which Rangers could have honoured his memory would have been doing their utmost to find and develop the next Ray Jones. In the end, financial problems of the club's own making forced them down that route and it's encouraging to see them trying hard now to make up for those years that were lost.

# 7

# WE SHOULDN'T GO CRAZY IN JANUARY SALES

## (December 2007)

It would be easy for me now, with the benefit of hindsight, to make the claim that I had serious misgivings about Flavio Briatore from day one. The truth is that, like everyone else, I didn't really know what to expect from QPR's new owner – or co-owner, strictly speaking – and I'd like to think I'm reasonable enough to afford anyone the benefit of the doubt unless they give me good reason to think otherwise.

With that said, there were a couple of factors that made me feel uneasy, as opposed to outright hostile, almost immediately after Briatore and Bernie Ecclestone had completed their takeover of the club. The first of those was the signing of Mikele Leigertwood from Sheffield United – a solid, experienced Championship player and capable of operating in more than one position. The transfer fee, on the other hand, left little change from £1m and, while that might sound a modest outlay in this day and age, let's try putting it into the context of where QPR were in autumn 2007.

Leigertwood's arrival cost Rangers far more than they had paid for any player during the previous decade. Only five players, in fact, had ever cost the club a bigger fee – and, apart from Roy Wegerle and Gavin Peacock, none of those could be described as representing value for money in the long term. No doubt many Rangers fans were delighted to see the cash being splashed again, but to me it raised questions about whether Briatore actually cared how wisely his investment was being spent.

Which brings me on to the second, and greater, cause for concern. The announcement that Gianni was to remain in his role as chairman – although he later took on the title of sporting director. On the one hand, the new owners might feel their lives would be made easier by keeping someone already familiar with the club on board. The flip side was this: how could they possibly think it wise to put Gianni in charge of buying and selling players, handing him a sizeable budget to do so, when his record over the last few years had been so abysmal? That suggested to me they hadn't done any kind of homework on the club's recent past – and it would eventually become clear they had no interest in the club's history, period.

Foreign ownership of English football clubs was, by then, becoming widespread. Some of the overseas investors have been good for the game, some have not. It would be impossible – and misleading – to tar them all with the same brush. While this may be an unpopular view, particularly as Fulham were the club in question, I always regarded Mohamed Al Fayed as a leading example of a foreign owner who behaved in the right way. By which I mean that Al Fayed never pretended to be an expert on running a football club, so he used his wealth to hire people who were – and let them get on with the job. Yes, there was the occasional PR disaster, such as the Michael Jackson statue at Craven Cottage, but by and large he didn't interfere and reaped the rewards by taking Fulham to the Premier League and establishing the club at the top level. It can be little coincidence that Fulham surrendered that status the year after Al Fayed had sold the club.

Unfortunately, the tone of reporting in national newspapers that surrounded Briatore's arrival at QPR didn't help matters at all in terms of managing expectations. Suddenly Rangers were being inaccurately referred to as 'the richest club in the world' and 'the Chelsea of the Championship' – hardly a label most fans would be keen to acquire! Briatore himself was widely ridiculed after being quoted as saying he expected the club to reach the Champions League within four years, a target that was hastily revised to explain he'd actually meant the Premier League. It served to confirm that his understanding of football was minimal – perfectly understandable, but once again highlighted why he should have turned to shrewd people who did know what was required in the English game.

It was clear that would not be the case as the vultures began to circle around John Gregory in those first few weeks. Gianluca Vialli, who was pictured in the directors' box at Loftus Road, did at least have experience of English football, unlike compatriot Alessandro Costacurta – also mentioned in dispatches as a leading candidate for the manager's job. I wrote a critique of Gregory's first year in charge, pointing out that he had recruited wisely the previous season and injected some fighting spirit into a ragged squad. At the same time, I felt he had done himself no favours by ignoring some players completely and repeatedly deploying others out of position.

With no wins from the first six league games – and no hard-luck stories either, to be truthful – it was only a matter of time before the new owners gave Gregory his cards, and he clearly knew that too. Which was why, I think, he was caught laughing by the TV cameras during the seventh game, an extremely one-sided 5-1 drubbing at West Brom – not because he found his team's capitulation amusing, but a rueful acknowledgement of his imminent fate.

While I waited by the players' tunnel to try and grab a post-match interview – which, in the circumstances, was never likely to prove a successful mission – I observed Gianni jabbering on his phone in Italian as he walked, grim-faced, towards the dressing room. The chairman's body language was clear confirmation of the subject under discussion, as well as the identity of the person on the other end of the line. Gregory, though, was calmness personified when he turned up for his post-match – or post-sacking – interview, with no real sign of emotion. One final 'All right, Benjy?' and he was gone. The club posted an official announcement the next morning, with Mick Harford taking over for the midweek game at Colchester – albeit with a strong indication from Gianni that he had little chance of being considered as a permanent appointment.

Harford actually remained in charge for the next four weeks, while the club tried and failed to entice former Udinese coach Francesco Guidolin to Loftus Road, and I must say I enjoyed dealing with him. Despite the hard man reputation he'd (deservedly) acquired during his playing days, Harford turned out to be very approachable and also recognised the value in speaking separately to the local media, which is always a good sign in my view. And he did a good job when it came to stabilising the ship, tightening up at the back as Rangers collected eight points from his five games.

Prior to the final match of Harford's tenure, a 1-0 win at Charlton, I did manage to catch up with Chris Powell again, thanks to a friend who was now working in the media department at The Valley. We chatted about his affection for QPR – while Chris openly identified as a Spurs fan, he viewed Rangers as his 'second' team – and also the summer of 2005, when I'd tried to help bring him to the club. It turned out that Ollie must have been keen enough to source his phone number from somewhere else, as they did eventually hold two or three conversations about a possible move to QPR! Chris admitted the deal had been 'quite close, but it never came off'.

Like most people outside Italy, I'd never heard of Luigi de Canio until his appointment as QPR coach – rather than manager, note – was announced on the Monday following the Charlton game. I rang Gerry Francis to get his reaction and even he admitted, 'I thought it must be Paolo di Canio, at first.' But overall Gerry's view of the new arrival was a positive one – as he pointed out, his old boss Dave Sexton, like De Canio, had joined QPR with no prior connection to the club and took them closer to winning the league than anyone else before or since. He also predicted that De Canio would want to recruit mostly Italian players as he would know more about them. Which would have been logical, if the new coach had indeed been tasked with player recruitment.

Unfortunately, there was no question about whose domain that continued to be and now, at least, the club were being completely open about it. A steady stream of players had continued to arrive on loan after Gregory's departure, all of them from within the English game, but it was clearly a scattergun approach. Namely, if you sign enough players then a certain percentage of them will work out. That, basically, became the QPR mantra over the next few years and remained embedded at the club even after Briatore and Ecclestone had moved on.

In fairness to Gianni, the bulk of his initial signings that autumn proved to be good value – the likes of Rowan Vine, Akos Buzsaky and Scott Sinclair were all exciting attacking players and provided the crowd with some entertainment, even if results were slow to improve. De Canio's first match in charge finished in a 2-0 win at home to Hull – curiously, identical to the result that had launched Gregory's reign – but there were no further victories in the next seven and Rangers continued to flounder around the relegation zone. The impact made by Vine and Buzsaky was balanced out by the performances of Bob Malcolm, certainly one of the worst players I have ever witnessed wearing a QPR shirt. The Sheffield Wednesday game where he made his debut was quite a challenge for me on commentary – while you certainly couldn't ignore Malcolm's obvious shortcomings, it was also unwise to go overboard about him on what was, after all, the club's in-house media.

In theory Malcolm, who'd signed on loan from Derby, was a central defender by trade. Now sometimes you watch a defender who doesn't have much pace, but does possess aerial strength. Or maybe he tackles efficiently, but isn't as aware as he needs to be in terms of positioning. It's like a game of Top Trumps, where players' attributes are evaluated as a mark out of 100 and normally the strengths and weaknesses balance each other out. But if I'd been responsible for drawing up the card displaying Malcolm's various attributes as a defender, he'd have scored single figures in each category. I recall David McIntyre telling me he'd quizzed Gianni about Malcolm's signing and was met with a shrug and a response along the lines of 'we had to get someone and I couldn't get anyone else'. David suggested that Fitz Hall, who was out of favour at Wigan at that time, might have been a better bet. 'Phil who?' Gianni enquired.

How did I get on with Gigi de Canio? I honestly can't say I did or didn't. It was impossible to establish any kind of relationship with him because of the language barrier. That might have improved if the coach had stayed at Loftus Road longer than six months – and, in any case, I often suspected his English was better than he let on. Initially, the club asked Marc Nygaard, who spoke Italian fluently, to accompany De Canio when he spoke to the media after the games, but they then hired a young man named Reuben to interpret for him. Poor Reuben always appeared rather ill at ease and that can't have been helped by the embarrassing situation that followed a match against Crystal Palace. De Canio's answer to a question was translated at length by Reuben, only to draw ire from the veteran Italian-speaking *Sunday Times* writer Brian Glanville, who interceded to bellow, 'That's not what he said at all!'

I was also somewhat amused by the presence of De Canio's two assistant coaches, Iuri Bartoli and Paolo Pavese. While a bit of internet research revealed that Iuri did have a coaching background, the same could not be said for Paolo, who seemed to wander vaguely around the training ground clutching a clipboard at times. He certainly didn't appear to have a great deal of coaching input, as far as I could see.

Later in the season, when De Canio had to return home due to a family bereavement, I was intrigued to learn that Gareth Ainsworth had been asked to take training in his absence. It was nice for Gareth, as a senior player with long-term coaching ambitions, to be given that recognition, and I was keen to ask him about it when we spoke for his next newspaper column.

'Obviously it's good experience for you,' I commented. 'Was it a surprise though? I mean, wouldn't they have asked the assistant coaches to stand in first?'

Gareth was a bit hesitant in his response. 'Er, well, I think it's just that Paolo hasn't actually done a lot of coaching before.'

I felt I had to press the point. 'So, when you said he hasn't done a lot of coaching before – has he done any coaching?'

There was a brief silence from Gareth, trying to work out what he could possibly say next, and eventually bursting into laughter before admitting, 'No, I don't think so.'

Eventually I tactfully suggested it might be best if we skipped over the subject of the non-playing ringer altogether, to which Gareth readily agreed. I never did discover exactly what Paolo's role at QPR was, beyond being a mate of De Canio's!

I missed seeing Rangers secure their second win under the new coach as I'd gone to stay with my cousins in New York – the first of many thoroughly enjoyable visits to the Big Apple. The game at Burnley, which should have taken place on the day of Ray Jones's death, was rearranged for a Tuesday night and that posed a problem. Arranging cover for a weekend match was usually straightforward, persuading friendly freelancers to hack to Turf Moor (no pun intended) in the middle of the week less so. In the end, I was very grateful to Ian Taylor – who presumably drew up the QPR media team rota but had handed himself the short straw on this one – for agreeing to step in and supply us with a match report. Ian had been a local newspaper reporter himself prior to joining the club, so he knew what we needed and didn't mind providing it.

Perhaps it's important to highlight that at this stage, just to stress that the relationship with the club and their media team remained a fairly close-knit one. However, I probably started the process of loosening those threads soon afterwards, although it would still be more than another year before the whole thing unravelled completely. I didn't really think about it at the time, but I now regret deciding to quit the commentary gig early in 2008 – it was hasty, impulsive and can't have done me a great deal of credit in Ian and Paul Morrissey's eyes.

The real reason I gave it up was because of a member of security staff at Loftus Road who totally epitomised the term 'jobsworth'. What I'd tended to do, particularly as the season advanced into the cold winter months, was to make my way back from the gantry at half-time, around the perimeter of the pitch and back along the tunnel to the press room in the South Africa Road Stand, for a much-needed takeaway cup of tea. Believe me, it could be chilly up there on a December evening! It worked out fine as long as I left on the half-time whistle and went straight round and back – I had a pass permitting me to take that route and nobody seemed to mind.

Until I ran into this guy. 'No,' he insisted. 'You can't go down the tunnel carrying liquid, it's against ground regulations.' After a few minutes of arguing fruitlessly, I abandoned the untouched cup on the floor and made for the tunnel, well aware that I had to be ahead of the teams returning for the start of the second half! Players don't tend to be accompanied by mascots after the half-time break, especially not flustered 30-somethings attempting to go around the pitch rather than on it.

But the jobsworth even objected to my giving up! 'You can't leave that there,' he declared with the flat certainty of the smug nit-picker who delights in winding people up. I told him I couldn't care less, or words to that effect, and began hurriedly making my way back to the gantry – hardly in the best frame of mind to resume the commentary.

It was unfortunate that I bumped into the jobsworth again after the match, while leaving the ground with Tony Incenzo. Just seeing him got me irate all over again and I informed him I would be making a complaint to the club about his behaviour. 'What behaviour would that be, sir?' he enquired calmly, with the deliberate use of 'sir' knowing, I'm sure, that he would appear polite in front of an audience while successfully enraging me further.

All of this must sound so trivial and, looking back, it was. I suppose all I can offer by way of explanation is that I felt so much a part of the club back then, it was as if someone who had appeared out of nowhere was suddenly telling me how to behave in my own home. Tony kept telling me, 'You were here before he was and you'll be here after he's gone.' Which was true. But I knew the guy was certain to carry on making things difficult for me after our double confrontation. I relayed the incident to Ian, who promised to follow it up with the relevant department, but ultimately there wasn't a lot they could do when the jobsworth doubtless insisted he was following rules and instructions. People like him always do.

However, I shouldn't have reacted as I did. Maybe I should have got into the habit of taking a thermos flask with me on matchdays! It certainly wasn't an insoluble problem and I must have looked childish and irrational by telling Ian I couldn't do the commentary any more. I tried to justify it by saying the club's circumstances had changed – whereas I'd been happy to do it for free when they couldn't afford to pay anyone, things were rather different now money appeared to be no object for the club's new owners. That was a terrible excuse and, being totally honest, it was a classic case of cutting my nose off to spite my face by giving up something I'd enjoyed doing so much.

Winding the clock back slightly to the end of 2007, QPR were, inevitably, featuring regularly in dispatches as the tabloids began to speculate about which players would be on the move when the January transfer window opened for business. All the ingredients were there – not only had Briatore's wealth been supplemented by the investment of Indian steel billionaire Lakshmi Mittal, fuelling the 'richest club in the world' tag, but Gianni would clearly continue to behave like the proverbial kid in a sweetshop.

Now, I should probably explain my general feelings about the transfer window – with regard to football in general, not just QPR. It astonishes me that sizeable numbers of football fans have come to view their club's transfer activity with importance at least equal to, if not greater than, performances on the field. Nowadays you frequently hear conversations taking place, among intelligent people, about whether such and such has 'had a good transfer window'. Eh? Whatever happened to evaluating the season itself? Isn't football about how many matches you've won, not how many players you've bought?

This kind of talk might be more understandable if it were actually about assessing a club's transfer business as a whole. But that's rarely the case. Notions of success or failure in the transfer window are usually defined by answering the question 'How many players did they sign?' and the higher the number, the greater the perceived success. If the answer is 'none', that can be deemed as proof of a lack of ambition, almost a dereliction of duty! Managers who fail to sign any players during the transfer window are regularly badgered by the media and lambasted by their fans. The generally accepted truism is that buying more players is always a good thing – questions are never asked about wasting money, or the logic of where a new arrival will fit into the existing squad.

I honestly believe much of this warped thinking comes from the computer simulation games fans love to play – admittedly so much more sophisticated than when I used to spend hours at a time, during my student days, absorbed in Championship Manager 2! It's simple in the virtual world – if you're under pressure from the board, the answer is always to sign more players. And if one of them scores a low rating in his first couple of games? No problem, you can go and sign an immediate replacement. It's as simple as that. A few clicks, scroll through the player's attributes, check the scouting report, put in the offer … and problem solved!

The real world isn't like that. Logically, you could argue that the fewer players a club signs in one go, the more they've been doing right. I'm not going to claim I never used to get excited about QPR signing a new player, far from it. Strikers especially generate a buzz among fans, keen to see them hitting the net for the first time. I loved watching Roy Wegerle make his Loftus Road debut against Coventry, John Spencer firing Rangers into the lead at Reading, Kevin Gallen's homecoming goal against Barnsley.

At the same time, it's worth remembering that one of QPR's most successful seasons in the modern era came in the inaugural Premier League of 1992-93. Top of the table after four games, fifth at the end of the season and highest-placed team in London, ahead of Arsenal and way ahead of Spurs and Chelsea. Exactly how many additions did Rangers make in the previous summer? One – Chester winger Brian Croft, who never made a league appearance for the club. The only player to arrive mid-season was centre-forward Devon White, who cost a small fee from Cambridge and went on to become something of a cult hero at Loftus Road. My point is that Rangers progressed by nurturing and improving the players that they already had – and that was an area where Gerry Francis, the manager at that time, excelled. Buying more and more players may always be a popular course of action, but that doesn't necessarily make it the right one.

So, whereas some QPR supporters probably awaited January 2008 with keen anticipation, I felt far more uneasy. The knowledge that Gianni would be supervising the feverish scramble to recruit as many players as soon as possible filled me with foreboding, given his generally woeful track record. I decided it was worth putting together a back page comment for the paper's Christmas edition, trying to take a positive tone towards the recent investment but stressing the importance of spending funds wisely. Watford's Gavin Mahon was one of the names touted for a January move and one of the questions I posed was whether he would represent a notable upgrade on either Adam Bolder or Mikele Leigertwood in the defensive midfield role. Bolder, let's not forget, had been at QPR for less than a year, Leigertwood for only four months!

*'There is no point in buying players just for the sake of it. A centre-back, a right-back, a left-sided midfielder and another forward should be sufficient to lift the team towards the top half of the table.*

*'The high turnover of players under a succession of managers in the last few years is one of the reasons Rangers have struggled in the Championship.*

*'These are exciting times for QPR. Let's just remember that the worst thing a starving man can do is gorge immediately on an enormous meal.'*

What I wrote was intended as a piece of temperate advice, an attempt to keep supporters from getting too carried away. Deep down, however, I knew perfectly well it would fall on deaf ears.

Sure enough, within days of the window opening, Mahon had been signed amidst a deluge of new faces as Ian Taylor's emails began to flood my inbox. Including permanent deals for three of the loan players – Buzsaky, Vine and Ephraim – Rangers had already made eight additions to their squad by the time they headed to Stamford Bridge for an FA Cup third-round meeting with Chelsea on the first weekend of the year.

Considering that upheaval, the team did well to restrict Chelsea to a single goal, which hit the post and rebounded in off Lee Camp. But, although defeat at Stamford Bridge is never ideal, just being there in numbers and watching a QPR side give a fair account of themselves did, I'm sure, offer supporters a tantalising glimpse of how it might feel to be filling Premier League away ends on a regular basis once more.

From a professional perspective, the regularity of incoming transfers meant a ready supply of player interviews with which to fill space. The new men were all willing to talk and the club were happy for them to do so. Of course, if they happened to mention one of the new buzzwords at Loftus Road – 'ambition' – in the course of those interviews, then better still for a club suddenly becoming conscious that they needed to hone their PR image. It was also just as well that so many players were available to chat, because, for reasons already explained, there wasn't much chance of having a conversation with De Canio unless Reuben was on hand to interpret and dilute it.

As for speaking to anyone at board level ... well, it quickly became clear that wasn't going to happen. I did ask Ian early on if he thought there'd be an opportunity to meet any of the new owners and he gave me an incredulous look, the sort of response that might have been appropriate if I'd requested a trip to Mars. It started to dawn on me that Briatore and his cohorts weren't remotely interested in ingratiating themselves with QPR supporters or the West London community – and certainly wouldn't deign to give a guy from the local rag the time of day.

But what had also changed was that Gianni suddenly became evasive and unwilling to speak to me around this time. He was still perfectly friendly, he'd always say hello if we happened to meet at a game or the training ground – but if I rang him it would be something along the lines of, 'Look, you know I can't tell you anything. This is not my club any more, it's other people running it.' I found that difficult to understand, not least because Gianni was quite frankly one of the least discreet individuals I've ever encountered, letting information slip to anyone, anywhere. Maybe he'd needed people like me during the previous few years, when he was trying to keep the fans onside and ultimately arrange the sale of the club, and now he didn't. Fair enough, I'd have accepted that if it weren't for the fact that he continued to feed information to Paul Warburton on a regular basis – hilariously quoted as 'a QPR insider' when the nature and tone of stories often made their source blindingly obvious! Admittedly, Warbo was probably a bit more persuasive than me and, because his approach to stories was often what you might call rather left-field, I saw him more as someone to work with rather than against. I rarely felt it was worth wasting time and energy in getting hung up about what rival publications were doing – sometimes you might have the better stories, at other times they will and the key concern should always be whether you're offering the reader anything different.

With that in mind, and given that QPR were observing their traditional blank date at the end of January (sometimes known as FA Cup fourth-round weekend), I took the opportunity to speaking to a former Rangers player who was still in the competition. Richard Pacquette, by then, was working at a school in Neasden as well as turning out for Havant & Waterlooville, who had beaten Swansea in the previous round to earn a tie against Liverpool. It was great to reminisce with Richard – even about the play-off final in Cardiff – and I was pleased that he ended up scoring at Anfield the following weekend.

Inevitably, perhaps, the Pacquette story prompted me to climb back onto one of my hobby horses – the ongoing demise of anything resembling a youth policy at Loftus Road. Amidst all the expensive arrivals that month – and, believe me, a £5m outlay represented big bucks for a struggling Championship club at the time – it was hard to ignore the fact that all the home-grown youngsters, with the exception of Angelo Balanta, had been ditched in one fell swoop. Pat Kanyuka, Shabazz Baidoo and Kieron St Aimie had all featured for the first team earlier in the season, now they'd been abruptly ushered towards the exit. The message, as far as I could see, was evident – we have no interest in developing our own players now we have the means to buy them from elsewhere. For me, that ran contrary to the ethos of the club I'd grown up supporting and I ran another comment piece on the back page, headlined 'What about tomorrow, Flavio?' and outlining what was, I suppose, my first public criticism of the new regime.

We were still at a stage, I think, where constructive criticism was more appropriate than outright condemnation. I hoped the piece might prompt some response from Rangers fans, and, sure enough, it did – a very mixed one. I printed a cross-section of the emails I received, all of which were well argued and ranged in tone from unease and foreboding to confidence in the people running the club. One reader opted for a 'wait-and-see' approach, saying he hoped my assessment was wrong and adding, 'If you are right then this will be a significant step in us losing our soul which, above all else, no real QPR supporter wants to see.'

I hoped I'd be proved wrong too.

# 8

# STAND UP, IF YOU LOVE RANGERS

### (September 2008)

Despite concerns about the overall direction in which I could see my club moving, there was no question that the quality of football at Loftus Road had climbed a few notches. Even after forsaking my vantage point in the Ellerslie Road gantry and reclaiming a seat in the press box directly opposite, I couldn't fail to enjoy the entertainment served up by QPR's new-look team. With Martin Rowlands pulling the strings in midfield, Akos Buzsaky and Rowan Vine setting up the chances and Patrick Agyemang finishing them off at an impressive rate, Rangers were soon moving up the table. The performances against Bristol City and Stoke – both resulting in 3-0 victories at Loftus Road – really stood out in that spring of 2008 and served to underline a point George Graham had made several years earlier. Namely that, as long as you perform on home turf, you'll keep the bulk of your fans on your side. Certainly there was no doubting the coach's popularity – he'd answer the call from the Loft with numerous waves during a match, triggered by a chorus of 'Gigi de Canio, Bernie and Flavio' to the tune of 'La Donna e Mobile'.

Agyemang's purple patch in front of goal got me thumbing through one of Gordon Macey's excellent QPR history books to work out the last time a Rangers player had netted in six consecutive matches. It turned out nobody had managed that feat since Rodney Marsh, more than four decades earlier, which formed the basis for a nice feature on Agyemang – although he assured me he didn't look at statistics or records. Players often downplay their achievements in that way, but I find it difficult to believe they don't keep track of the stats to some degree. Unless, like Danny Shittu, they view football purely as a job and no more!

I also ran an interview with another of the January arrivals, left-back Damien Delaney, who I'd asked about his hopes of playing for Ireland. His actual reaction when I mentioned the subject was, 'Jesus. That'd be unbelievable!' – almost as if the idea of catching Giovanni Trapattoni's eye had never occurred to him. I was delighted when Delaney received his first call-up at the end of the season ... no doubt someone must have forwarded *the Times* story to the Republic manager.

I was still able to visit the training ground at Harlington on a fairly regular basis and it so happened I was in attendance when Rowan Vine had his leg broken in a challenge by American goalkeeper Matt Pickens, who had joined the club as short-term back-up. Poor Vine was carried off the training pitch, clearly in pain, and Paul Morrissey asked me not to publicise what I'd seen for the time being. I promised him I wouldn't – and I didn't, but incidents like that do have a habit of leaking into the public domain by one means or another and, sure enough, the news of Vine's injury appeared on one of the fans' forums later that day.

De Canio knew me by sight, if not by name, and seemed happy to have a conversation at the training ground – albeit by prior arrangement and via the interpreter. It wasn't the same as I'd been used to before, but that was probably inevitable and I was still able to record some semblance of the coach's thoughts on the squad and plans for next season. There certainly wasn't any indication that he might not stay to oversee what the owners clearly expected to be a promotion challenge.

Ah yes, the owners. It started to become clear towards the end of the season what we in the media could expect in future – a much more corporate tone, with flashy, over-embellished press conferences organised by PR companies who relentlessly pushed terminology such as 'brand' and 'project'. The first of these such events was held in March to announce QPR's new kit deal with Lotto Sport Italia and I'm not sure whether I was invited to attend or not, but either way I didn't go. I dutifully ran an item about the deal, complete with posed photo of Briatore on the pitch alongside two of the players, but it all made me feel uncomfortable – the whole thing smacked of trying to turn QPR into something they weren't and that theme would be repeated over and over again.

A few weeks later, the Loftus Road crowd were treated to more of the same before the final game of the season, against West Brom. Yes, another opportunity for Briatore to strut around on the pitch, this time surrounded by QPR legends such as Stan Bowles, Gerry Francis, Les Ferdinand and Paul Parker for the launch of the club's new crest! Two things struck me at the time. One, I didn't like the crest – it bore little resemblance to anything that had gone before in Rangers' history, and the unwieldy, complex design, topped off by a crown, just screamed arrogance and conceit. Those kind of gestures look ridiculous when you've as yet achieved nothing on the pitch to justify them. And second – who would call the club's logo a 'crest' anyway? Surely it's a badge, no more or less. It was certainly known as a badge when I used to collect the foil versions for my Panini sticker albums as a kid.

As it turned out, the unloved badge wouldn't be the only dramatic change taking place at the club during the close season. Within days of the West Brom game, De Canio was on his way back to Italy without explanation – and, as I discovered, the players were given strict instructions not to speak publicly about his departure. It was clear, however, that whether he'd been sacked or resigned, De Canio's exit had been on the cards for some time – shown by the unexpected speed with which QPR appointed his successor. And, speaking personally, I was pleasantly surprised when the new manager – not coach, this time – was confirmed to be Iain Dowie.

I'd always been impressed from afar by Dowie's managerial qualities. He struck me as a great thinker about the game, good at organising teams and, apart from a short, ill-fated spell at Charlton, overseeing a general improvement. I'd met him once or twice during his previous spell at QPR, and in many ways he'd been unlucky not to get the manager's job after Gerry Francis stood down. Overall I would argue that Ollie was the right man for the club at that time, because of the raw passion he brought to the role. But now, I felt, Dowie was the right man for the club – he was an experienced Championship manager with good knowledge of the English game. That seemed more relevant than nationality – there's no reason at all why a foreign manager with previous experience of English football shouldn't be successful. Fast-forwarding a number of years, I believed Rangers should have tried to lure Roberto Martinez when he was coming towards the end of his time at Wigan instead of leaping blindly into bed with Mark Hughes and then Redknapp, purely on the basis of being high-profile managers who happened to be available.

One thing Dowie had done during his brief stay at Charlton was to sign Simon Walton – so I thought it'd be worth picking up the phone to one of Rangers' forgotten men to see what he made of the appointment. It seemed an eternity since Walton had broken his leg in that pre-season friendly against Fulham – not so much a case of water under the bridge as bridges being burnt and rebuilt in a completely different style. He'd finished the season on loan at Hull, who were about to head to Wembley for the Championship play-off final, but was keen to try and rekindle his career at Loftus Road – something he'd never really had the chance to do.

Walton said all the right things and I wished him luck in his aspirations, but I'm sure he was under no illusions about the size of the task when it came to forcing his way into Dowie's team. Inevitably, the transfer machine had already begun whirring, with Spurs goalkeeper Radek Cerny and defender Peter Ramage, from Newcastle, the first to arrive. Fortunately for me, David McIntyre usually had his finger on the pulse when it came to that sort of thing and I relied heavily on him to help me out with back-page stories that summer while I tried to deal with two family bereavements in quick succession. But for David, it would have been a lot harder to keep up to date, given that I didn't have Dowie's phone number and Gianni was more reluctant to let things slip than had previously been the case. Strictly speaking, that wasn't true – he just wasn't letting things slip in my direction any more.

Although QPR tended to be the focus of the lead story on the back page more often than not, my view was always that you should treat everything on its own merits, and if there was a more newsworthy alternative it ought to take precedence. That proved to be the case a number of times during 2008, with Harlesden boxer James DeGale quite rightly taking up plenty of column inches as he qualified for the Beijing Olympics and went on to win the gold medal in the middleweight division. QPR did later try to 'claim' DeGale as one of their own, latching on to the fact he was also Lee Cook's second cousin! James didn't seem to mind going along with it, making the obligatory appearance at Loftus Road – although we'd established some time ago it was actually his grandfather, rather than him, who'd held a torch for Rangers. Later, after he'd turned pro and ended up as a world champion, James was more inclined to go and watch football at the Emirates as his trainer, Jim McDonnell, was a massive Arsenal fan. Oddly enough, though, I associate Loftus Road with James DeGale's Olympic success, as I remember watching the final on TV in the press room just before QPR's game against Doncaster. I turned to Warbo and remarked, 'Well, that's both of our back pages sorted for next week.' To my astonishment, Warbo admitted that wouldn't be the case for his paper – he was apparently expected to lead with a football story come what may! I really couldn't believe they'd deny top billing to a local boy who had just become an Olympic champion, but it wasn't my business. I suppose I should have counted myself lucky that I was basically afforded the freedom to fill the sports section in whatever way I chose.

That being the case, I was occasionally able to delegate tasks I didn't fancy all that much. Before anyone takes that statement as evidence of a cavalier, work-shy attitude, I suppose it needs some clarification! Doing the research, making the calls, writing up the interviews, sourcing the images and designing the pages – never a problem. In fact, more often than not, a pleasure. But when it came to attending another of the tedious, overblown press conference circuses arranged by Briatore's PR people – No, thank you. I'll be giving that a swerve if at all possible.

This time, they'd decided to hold it at Somerset House – heaven knows why. Presumably the central London venue was more convenient for Briatore or the representatives of Gulf Air, whose newly announced sponsorship deal with QPR was the pretext for all the pomp and circumstance. Anyway, I asked Ben Pearce – at that time the youngest and newest member of the sports team but someone who became a very trusted and valued colleague over the next nine years – if he'd mind going along instead. Ben duly obliged, sifting through all the PR bluster and guff to put together a decent story as Briatore revealed his three-year 'project' to take Rangers into the Premier League. Of course, that long-term goal would eventually become infamous under the banner of the 'Four Year Plan', with the bulk of the previous season being counted as the first of those four.

Many readers, whether QPR supporters or not, have probably watched the Four Year Plan documentary at some stage, so I won't touch on it to any great extent. What I will say is that I eventually saw the programme many years later and there was nothing in it that surprised or shocked me, being only too well aware of the way the club was run during the period in question. I was actually interviewed by the programme-makers after Rangers' first game of the 2008-09 season against Barnsley, and while I didn't mind giving praise where it was due I also stressed the need for the owners to be mindful of the club's history and fanbase if they wanted their 'project' to work. Not really the message of uncompromised support they were looking for, I'd imagine, so it wasn't too much of a surprise that my contribution ended up on the cutting-room floor!

For now, my guiding principle remained one of qualified, if not uncompromised, backing for the new-look QPR. That was the reason I decided to look at producing a pull-out supplement to mark the start of the season – it was something the *Recorder* had done for West Ham on an annual basis and I felt it might be worth running something similar on Rangers. The sales team got to work, with the Springbok pub sponsoring the back page and several other local businesses buying advertising space, and I set about filling the supplement with some editorial content. Overall, the theme was very much in tune with the progressive image the club were seeking to harness – I headed the front page 'Lucky 13?', referring to the number of seasons since Rangers had dropped out of the Premier League and, after gritting my teeth, included the new crest as well. We included interviews with Dowie, Cerny and Ramage, as well as a piece with the new deputy managing director Ali Russell, talking about the club's commercial tie-ups and doing his best to explain the controversial rise in ticket prices that had just been introduced. The centre pages were largely devoted to a picture spread that showcased the new QPR kit and the changes that had been made to Loftus Road over the summer – the lick of paint was very welcome, with mounted TV screens at either end of the ground. Apart from a large version of the crest slap-bang in the middle of the Ellerslie Road roof, I couldn't really grumble.

The only element of the supplement that might have been coolly received by the regime was my interview with former QPR captain Steve Morrow. The ex-Northern Ireland player might not have seemed an obvious choice to talk about Rangers' prospects, but I thought it was worth recalling how things had panned out the last time the club had spent money a decade earlier. Morrow had been one of the big-name players brought to Loftus Road with the aim of challenging for promotion, but instead ended up fighting a relegation battle – again, it seemed to me that lessons could be learned. If anyone was interested in listening, of course!

Gathering material for the supplement, as well as the actual sports section, meant making sure I got myself to a number of pre-season games. Stevenage wasn't too far up the road, but Rangers' tour of Scotland was a slightly different matter. Although I'd been north of the border a number of times, I'd yet to visit a Scottish football ground – so where better to begin than Falkirk? Crazy though it might sound, I accepted Tony Incenzo's invitation to join him on a day trip – yes, a day trip – to see QPR take on the Bairns. That involved something of a Planes, Trains and Automobiles itinerary, departing on a morning flight to Glasgow and returning in the evening from Edinburgh. It all worked out fine until the last part – we had lunch in the town, made our way to the stadium in good time and watched Rangers lose 2-0, after which I was able to chat with the new goalkeeper, Cerny. Unfortunately, though, our return flight was delayed until around 11pm – and Edinburgh airport is the kind of place where you run out of things to do within 20 minutes. At least it gave me the opportunity to start writing up the Cerny interview, if nothing else. And, as I've said before, it's never a bad thing to show your face at a far-flung away venue – managers, coaches and players do tend to notice who turns up to cover these games.

Before the new season got under way, we had to endure yet another of Briatore's ludicrous press conferences to announce what his PR people considered sensational news. Which, of course, meant it wasn't. Briatore was bent on publicising the fact that he was friends with Real Madrid's president, Ramon Calderon – maybe he thought that strengthened his non-existent football credentials in some way – and had decided QPR would sign one of Real's youngsters, Dani Parejo, on loan. In fairness to Parejo, he went on to have a very decent career with Valencia and eventually won a handful of caps for Spain. But at that time, he was a teenager that Rangers really didn't need for any footballing reason. Poor Ian Taylor had to try and drum up interest among the local media for this event, which at least was being held at Loftus Road this time. As well as sending out the email invitation, he also rang me up to see if I was planning to attend.

'No offence, Ian, but it really isn't worth my time,' I told him. That wasn't meant to sound arrogant, just a statement of fact – I had a lot to get through the next day and using up two or three hours on what was effectively a non-story didn't seem like a great idea.

Smart thinking on Mr Taylor's part, though. 'You know we're re-signing Lee Cook as well – how about if I get him to come along too and have a word with the local boys?'

Sold. Of course that was worth my while! So I came along, sat through Briatore's nonsense and then went to catch up with Lee Cook while the owner, arm around Parejo, was posing for photos in the centre circle. The back page that week was all about Cookie's return to Loftus Road, while Parejo got three or four lines.

Another notable aspect of that press conference was that Dowie slipped in late and stood at the back while Briatore held court at the top table. Quite significant when you think about it – how often do you see a team manager completely uninvolved in the announcement of a new player's arrival? That in itself made it abundantly clear that Dowie had not had any say whatsoever in the Parejo signing and he confirmed that when one of my media colleagues invited him to comment. 'As long as I'm in charge of team selection, that's the Holy Grail for me,' was the manager's assessment. It wouldn't be long before it dawned on Dowie that he wasn't in charge of that either.

Rumours were already circulating of a bust-up between manager and owner ahead of the Barnsley match, but Dowie took his place in the dugout and managed to guide his side to a shaky 2-1 victory. It was no surprise whatsoever when Barnsley took an early lead – Rangers were there to be taken down a peg after the ridiculous way the club had approached the occasion. Fireworks, dancing girls – all part of the overblown pre-match spectacle that might be justified at a club beginning their defence of the Premier League title, not at a mid-table Championship club that had achieved absolutely nothing. If I'd been a Barnsley player, that would be all the motivation I'd have needed. 'Just who do they think they are?' I'd have been asking myself.

If I had to choose one phrase to sum up the Briatore regime, it would be 'all style and no substance'. Hype, glitz and glamour were copious – there was rarely anything concrete to back those up. One example was the steep increases in ticket prices at Loftus Road – having already hiked the costs of season tickets during the summer, the club then raised matchday prices five or six weeks into the season, with some seats costing £50 a go. That was the kind of rate you might have expected to pay at Arsenal around that time.

I found it utterly outrageous, as did many other QPR fans. Traditionally, the club's fanbase had been fairly working-class – but those figures risked pricing established supporters out of the market altogether. It seemed that Briatore was perfectly content to do that – those fans weren't the kind who reflected the image he was so determined to present.

Worse followed in September when the club made it clear they weren't only planning to fleece QPR fans – suddenly they announced that Derby County supporters would also be charged £50 apiece for the privilege of watching their team at Loftus Road! Eventually, the Football League intervened and Briatore backed down, but the damage to the club's reputation was well and truly done. I spoke to Ali Russell again, hopeful in a sense that he'd be able to offer some kind of convincing explanation and reassurance about what was going on. Although Ali had a sympathetic manner and a slick turn of phrase that would, I suspect, have made him a successful politician if he'd chosen to take that route, he struggled to defend the policy. 'We feel we're offering value for money, providing a good entertainment product,' was about as much as he could muster.

The Derby debacle also, I felt, was part of another alarming trend. When I'd been growing up, QPR were a team that many supporters of other clubs held genuine affection for. I had friends who were Brentford or Spurs fans, but didn't mind coming along to enjoy a game at Loftus Road now and then. Briatore's behaviour had begun to alter the landscape. I became aware that more people were beginning to dislike QPR, and, while some dismissed that as economic envy, it was far more about the image of arrogance and greed the club's owners projected and their evident contempt for ordinary football fans.

While it was far less important than the ticket-pricing policy, the 'style over substance' motif also manifested itself in a more personal issue – the catering for the media on matchdays! I must stress I have no time for certain journalists who swan around with an enormous sense of entitlement and think it's appropriate to post images of their free lunch on social media. And, incidentally, might be better advised to cut down on their food intake altogether! But nevertheless I was completely unimpressed by the changes QPR made in the kitchen at the start of that season.

To be honest, the press room catering at Loftus Road had never been that great. A couple of plates of sandwiches that were often past their best and a few digestives to accompany the tea and coffee – that was usually the fare on offer. Nobody should take umbrage at that – some clubs pull out all the stops to feed visiting journalists, others don't provide anything beyond tea, coffee and bottles of water. That's how it is. My personal feeling is that clubs should probably provide more for evening than afternoon games, on the basis you might not be leaving the ground before about 11pm and are likely to be a bit peckish well before that time.

Anyway, QPR had decided to sweep away the plates of tired sandwiches and replace them with caterers from an Italian restaurant in the West End. As a result, two or three heated trays were set up in the press room, each filled with some kind of pasta dish. Which might sound fine – except that the fare was invariably Bolognese or some other kind of meat-based dish and that's not of much interest if, like me, you've been a vegetarian for most of your life. Alternatively, maybe you're vegan, or have specific dietary needs on religious or medical grounds. Well, tough luck. Because, aside from this one dish, there was nothing else to eat whatsoever! Not a sandwich, not a biscuit. It reminded me of the Fawlty Towers guest who surveys the gourmet night menu to find one item listed – 'So what do you do, if you don't like duck?'

'Er, if you don't like duck, you're rather stuck,' Basil replies with an uneasy chuckle. That summed up my situation too! I made enquiries to see if there might be anything else on the menu, but it clearly hadn't occurred to the caterers – or the club – that not everyone would be able to tuck into their one dish. Now, I appreciate this may not seem a matter of massive importance to everyone – but I found it extremely irritating and, yes, unacceptable. I know Tony Incenzo and I will always disagree on this – he still lauds the catering as fantastic and maybe, from his perspective, it was. From mine, it was non-existent and another example of how the reality was often totally at odds with the club's image during the Briatore years.

Dealing with Dowie, at least, was an absolute pleasure – albeit, only for a matter of months. He was calm and straight-talking, didn't duck questions and it was something of a relief not to endure John Gregory's whim of keeping you hanging around at the training ground for an hour or more. Not only was Dowie willing to discuss QPR matters, he also spent some time talking to me about his memories of Hendon – the club where he'd originally made his name as a player and one of the non-league sides we covered in the paper each week. Having said all that, I didn't get to know Dowie well enough that I automatically recognised his voice on the phone.

That enabled Paul Morrissey to execute a perfect wind-up on me one morning. It was during the build-up to Rangers' away game at Coventry, where Dowie had been manager the previous year, so I'd asked Paul if I could have a word with him about going back to the Ricoh Arena for the first time. That's a fairly standard angle for match previews, so I didn't anticipate any problem and sure enough Paul rang up to say he was with the manager and would pass the phone over for me to ask some questions.

Except – he only pretended to pass the phone over. To my surprise, 'Dowie' was absolutely bursting with football clichés all of a sudden … 'It's just another game to me, Ben' … 'All about the three points' … 'Anyone can beat anyone else in the Championship.' Wondering how on earth I was going to make this sound vaguely interesting, I did my best to soldier on with the interview until Paul eventually started laughing and admitted Dowie was busy on another call. Top marks to Paul, who, as I'd found out on other occasions, could be totally convincing when he was in the mood for pranks. And he did put the real Iain Dowie on the phone a few minutes later – at least, I think he did!

For me, Dowie was doing a good job as manager – and I firmly believe he would have taken QPR to a top-six finish that season. I went to Villa Park at the end of September for the third round of the Carling Cup, and Rangers' 1-0 win, courtesy of a Damion Stewart header, was a real triumph of organisation and tactical skill. What also shouldn't be overlooked is that the victory over Villa was the first time QPR had beaten a Premier League side since losing their own top-flight status. In my view, that was a significant stepping stone, a hint that it might not be impossible to compete again with the big boys of English football at some stage in the near future. And of course the draw for the next round handed Rangers an even more attractive prize – a trip to Old Trafford was something every supporter would look forward to. As for the league – a return of 18 points from 12 games was more than promising and, when Dowie was sacked, the team were ninth in the table. To put it into context, that was higher than QPR had finished since 1997, so hardly a failure by the standards of anyone who understood football.

Critics of Dowie's may argue that the football was too functional at times, a contrast with some of the free-flowing stuff served up in the second half of the previous season. What I would point out is that the one weakness in the squad at the time was a dearth of reliable goalscorers. Dowie made it clear that he'd asked Gianni to sign a striker on loan, but no such player ever materialised. Instead, the manager was landed with Damiano Tommasi, who'd had an impressive career with Roma but was now 34 and short of match fitness. Oh, and operated as a defensive midfielder – a position for which Dowie already had three or four options.

'He was available and he was happy to come to London,' was the manager's response when asked about Tommasi – the absence of any further endorsement making it quite clear, again, that the player had arrived at Briatore's behest, nothing more. It was becoming harder and harder to disguise or ignore the owner's blatant interference in team affairs – even more so when Lee Camp was packed off on loan to Nottingham Forest a few weeks later.

I remember sitting in Dowie's office and asking him about the Camp situation, when Gianni had publicly stated that the goalkeeper was available for transfer. 'I haven't put him on the transfer list,' replied Dowie, with particular stress on the word 'I'. That came as no surprise – I found it hard to imagine anyone with any football knowledge would have been anxious to part with one of the Championship's best goalkeepers. Others may disagree, but for my money Camp was always a superior player to the somewhat limited Cerny. Briatore thought otherwise, however, so Camp had to go. I rang Adam Bolder – another player whose status at the club had altered just as swiftly – to get his view on Camp's fall from grace. Because Bolder was still officially a QPR player at that stage, he probably wasn't able to say as much as he'd have liked, although he did make the observation, 'That's just the way the club is at the moment. People have their own opinions.'

I wasn't able to get to Swansea for the midweek 0-0 draw that turned out to be Dowie's last game in charge, but I was aware that rumours of the manager's departure were beginning to gather pace once more. A couple of days later, I was on my way to Barnet Hospital for a physiotherapy session – having recently recovered from knee surgery – when a friend texted me to say the news had been confirmed. I'd hoped it wouldn't be true, both because I rated Dowie as a manager and because this felt, for me, like a real turning point in my relationship with QPR.

I'd been uneasy for quite some time about what QPR were turning into under Briatore. But Dowie's dismissal validated my suspicion that the owner was an irredeemably malign and destructive influence on the club and not enough people were speaking up about that. This was the point where I resolved to try and be one of those who did.

# 9

# PLAY-OFF...
# OR PAY-OFF?

### (March 2009)

Because Iain Dowie's sacking had been announced on a Thursday, I had several days to think about how to react. Although it may sound hard to believe, at this stage I still wasn't able to upload content to the newspaper's website unless I happened to be in the office! Instead of which, I was working on strengthening exercises with my physiotherapist. So I waited to see what, if anything, would happen over the weekend, when Rangers were playing Reading at the Madejski Stadium – under the leadership of Gareth Ainsworth. That, to be honest, was my immediate cause for concern – by putting Gareth in temporary charge, Briatore had just cost me a columnist!

Despite his elevation to player-coach under Dowie, Gareth had continued to make himself available for our weekly column up to that point. It worked well in that he was able to give a slightly different perspective on the team's performances, while also reminding readers that he was still a member of the playing squad and keen to get his boots on. But I realised immediately it would be impossible for him to continue now – apart from anything else, as the caretaker manager, he'd now be required to put his name to a column in the match programme for the foreseeable future. Having rung Gareth to thank him and wish him well in his new role, I wrote a few lines explaining that the column would be suspended for the time being. Reluctantly, I concluded there was little chance of finding a replacement among the rest of the playing squad – for the simple reason that you could no longer be certain of anyone remaining part of the playing squad for more than a few months!

Over the next few days, inevitably, there was plenty of tabloid speculation as to who would succeed Dowie. Zinedine Zidane and Terry Venables were two of the names bandied around and a number of people I spoke to – friends, football fans, fellow journalists – were keen to know what I thought. My response? Maybe a surprising one, maybe it seemed overly cynical – 'It really makes no difference,' I said. By now, it was beyond doubt that Briatore decided which players arrived, which players left and which players made the team. So all he actually wanted was someone to take training at Harlington – and then take the rap when the team failed to sweep all before them.

So that, basically, was the theme of my next back page. I felt it was the right time to adopt a less serious tone and concentrate on underlining how unreasonable and ridiculous the man at the top really was. So I tinkered around with Photoshop and superimposed Briatore's face on an image of a circus ringmaster, headlining the story 'Hats in the ring?' I suggested Kevin Keegan might be a perfect choice to take over – at the time, he'd recently opened a football centre in Scotland and called it the Soccer Circus. In case a further dose of sledgehammer subtlety was needed, I also printed a photograph of Briatore and Ainsworth together with the caption, 'The man in charge of team selection … alongside caretaker-manager Gareth Ainsworth'. That, by the way, wasn't intended to be disrespectful to Gareth – nobody could blame him for seizing the opportunity to prove his coaching credentials, even though I've no doubt he knew he certainly couldn't expect to be left to his own devices.

I genuinely think Gareth was in line to get the job permanently at one point. He guided the team to a point at Reading and solid home wins against Birmingham and Cardiff, as well as overseeing what might be considered a respectable 1-0 defeat to Manchester United in the Carling Cup. In truth, the fact that United relied on a late Carlos Tevez penalty to win the tie didn't tell the full story – namely, that QPR never looked remotely like threatening to score themselves. However, no doubt Briatore enjoyed the opportunity to rub shoulders with the Glazers and their other guests in the Old Trafford boardroom – which had always been the main motivation behind his decision to invest in QPR.

On this one, I'd have to say I was broadly in agreement with Briatore. It was several years since I'd had the chance to visit Old Trafford and I won't deny I thoroughly enjoyed the occasion, staying up in Manchester overnight and emailing copy for one of my colleagues to deal with the next morning. The Old Trafford tie was also the first time I (briefly) met Amit Bhatia, who represented his father-in-law, the steel tycoon Lakshmi Mittal, on the board – and it was hard not to be impressed by him. Slick, stylish, but also very much in touch with the QPR fans – in fact, he was off to join some of them for drinks in Manchester later that evening! Amit had already intervened over the unpopular ticket price rises, helping convince the owners to backtrack, and was clearly a man already in possession of the PR skills Briatore had no interest in acquiring.

While even the ringmaster may not have expected his team to beat Manchester United, he clearly did expect them to win every game at Loftus Road, particularly if he happened to be entertaining visiting celebrities such as Naomi Campbell. I can't recall who happened to be alongside Briatore in the directors' box for the game against Burnley a few days later, but the visitors ran out more comfortable winners than the 2-1 scoreline suggested, and that, it seemed, was enough to change his mind about Gareth.

Then, all of a sudden, the name of Paulo Sousa emerged a few days later. I vaguely recalled him playing for Juventus in the mid-1990s, but I can't truthfully say I knew a lot about the Portuguese – and the picture agency we used didn't seem to either. The most recent image of Sousa I could find was a very youthful version, turning out for his national team some years earlier, but that would have to do until he pitched up to his first match in charge of QPR at Watford.

It was around this time that Rangers' website completed its transformation into little more than a propaganda machine. Of course, the purpose of any company website is to present the organisation it represents in the most favourable light possible – that's self-explanatory. But some of the 'official' statements that QPR were now putting out, in terms of content and tone, seemed thoroughly bizarre – sometimes contradicting themselves as they strove to push a thinly disguised message. That game at Watford was a case in point, with Rangers announcing that their newly-appointed head coach – back to that title after the pretence of Dowie being 'manager' – would be in charge for the first time. Sousa looked on from the stands at Vicarage Road as his new side put in a shambolic display and were dismantled 3-0 by a Watford team struggling for form themselves. A few weeks later, however, the club had clearly decided that game should be retrospectively scrubbed from Sousa's record – taking pains to stress that their 1-0 defeat at Sheffield Wednesday was the first time the team had lost under the new coach. Apparently Gareth had been in charge after all, as had seemed to be the case at the time.

Well, so you might have thought. By the time Sousa fell from favour in the spring, the club had readjusted their 'official' record once more and the blame for that Watford defeat was heaped firmly at his door! In a way it was no surprise – some years later I learned that many of Ian Taylor's draft statements on club affairs were rejected by Briatore or his cohorts, with orders issued for a complete rewrite. No wonder, then, that there was a lack of consistency as well as transparency.

I found it outrageous that the owners couldn't even be bothered to thank Sheila Marson for her long service to the club when they fired her towards the end of 2008. Not a word of appreciation and certainly no attempt at an explanation. But I can't imagine they would have found much use for an experienced administrator who didn't fit in with the 'brand' they claimed to be building. No, far more important to appoint a Japanese lady as the club's 'Global Ambassador in the Far East' for this brand!

Out of all the absurd QPR statements that besmirched my inbox, the one that introduced Mrs Yuko Yamazaki took some beating. This mysterious lady, apparently a long-term business associate of Briatore's, had been invited to 'build the brand' in Japan and South Korea. I'm sure it would have been fascinating to hear her attempts to do that. Imagine the initial conversations: 'So this is a team from the English Premier League?' 'Er, no.' 'Right, but they're going into the Premier League next year?' 'Probably not.' 'But they have won titles before?' 'They won one cup, 40 years ago.'

What Briatore never seemed to understand was that, while all the boasting and ambitious talk might impress some in the business world, football is different. If you can't back up your pretensions of glory on the field of play, football fans – and the wider football community – will regard you as something of a joke. That, unfortunately, is what QPR were fast becoming and I hated seeing it happen. When it came to news value, Mrs Yamazaki's appointment was beneath contempt – not even worth a cursory couple of lines in my view.

Far more important, I felt, to focus on the instability Briatore was creating at the club and the effect that had on the players as well as the fans. I spoke to Hogan Ephraim following the Vicarage Road debacle and he voiced some frustration, making the point that, despite having spent slightly over a year at QPR, he'd already played under six different managers!

'To be quite honest, that's crazy,' Hogan said. 'You don't want to be walking into the changing room and no one knows what's happening from one day to the next. We keep saying 'it's a tight unit, a family' and then it breaks up every so often because the manager's gone.'

*One of the players I particularly admired when growing up was Ray Wilkins – in fact I later modelled my hairstyle on QPR's midfield maestro.*

*It wasn't too hard to manage a smile for my disembodied picture byline in the Recorder… this particular West Ham defeat was a welcome one!*

# Lack of creativity leaves Hammers second best

**QUEENS PARK RANGERS 1
WEST HAM UTD 0
Ben Kosky reports
from Loftus Road**

**PASSION, hard work and team spirit ... all these terms are frequently to be found in the vocabulary of Rangers boss Ian Holloway. It looks as if West Ham need to take a leaf out of his phrasebook.**

Yes, the Hammers were unlucky to be missing so many key players at one time, but the side they fielded should still have been capable of taking some reward from Saturday's London derby.

Instead, they proved that, despite the size of the squad Alan Pardew has assembled, the simultaneous absence of Teddy Sheringham and Matthew Etherington leaves the team severely shorn of creative tal-

*(L-R) Akos Buzsaky, Patrick Agyemang and Rowan Vine – three of the men who made QPR an attractive team to watch under their first foreign coach, Gigi de Canio.*

*Buzsaky and Hogan Ephraim (R) were both among the first – of numerous – permanent signings when the transfer window opened in January 2008.*

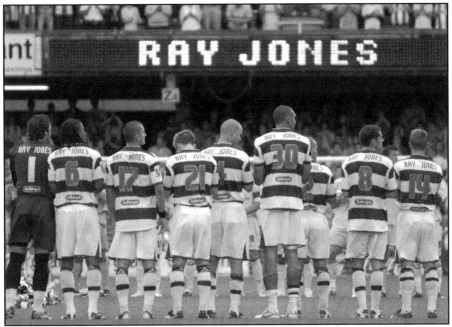

*One of the saddest times at Loftus Road... every QPR shirt bears the name of Ray Jones in tribute to their late team-mate before kick-off against Southampton in August 2007.*

*Rangers supporters also paid their respects to the 18-year-old striker, who had died in a car accident a week earlier.*

*Alejandro Faurlin (R) looks pleasantly surprised at what must surely have been a long-range strike by Mikele Leigertwood – Mikele didn't really do tap-ins!*

*Faurlin, in action here against Sheffield United, proved to be one of QPR's better signings during this period. Unfortunately, his transfer would be memorable for different reasons…*

*Flavio Briatore's antics gave me plenty of opportunities to play around with Photoshop on the Times back pages, as the club rapidly descended into farce. One of their classic moments was this promotion of season-ticket deals (below) with an image of Dexter Blackstock… a few days after Briatore had sent him packing to Nottingham Forest.*

The straw that broke the camel's back: after this uncomplimentary editorial comment about Flavio in September 2009, I was placed on the QPR blacklist.

Gareth Ainsworth was the supreme professional, both as a player and as a newspaper columnist, and it's no surprise to see the success he's enjoyed since going into management.

Picture: Dave Brennan

*No disrespect intended to Dani Parejo, who's gone on to have a good career – but his arrival highlighted the unsavoury transformation of QPR into a club where players could be signed and sold purely to satisfy Briatore's ego.*

*Once the man with the tinted glasses took a dislike to Dexter Blackstock, he had to go – despite being just about the only QPR player capable of finding the net during the 2008/09 season.*

*Dexter evades the Bristol City defence to fire home in Rangers' 1-1 draw at Ashton Gate earlier that season.*

*Molineux always seemed chilly, but it actually snowed at this game in late March, where QPR and Wolves shared the points in a 3-3 draw.*

For me, speaking to the players was even more essential now as the lines of communication to the manager/coach's office had gone dead again. It wasn't a language problem, as had been the case in Di Canio's day, and I was never sure whether Sousa himself was reluctant to speak to the regulars, or whether the club actively persuaded him not to. For whatever reason, though, aside from fulfilling his post-match duties – which could be as stultifying as some of the matches themselves – he just didn't seem to be available. Gareth had remained as part of the coaching set-up, of course, but he wasn't really in a senior enough position now to be speaking on the main man's behalf.

On this occasion, Warbo had found it just as impossible to talk to Sousa and eventually we combined forces after one home match, approaching the coach in reception as he was on his way out of the ground. Sousa seemed genuinely surprised to learn we'd been keen to sit down with him and invited us to come along to his office at Harlington after training one day the following week, which we did. He was polite and personable, even if he did have a habit I found rather irritating – specifically, making numerous references to 'the project' at QPR. By no means was Sousa the sole culprit when it came to that kind of thing – but for me, to hear the club described as a project was like a red rag to a bull. The implication of the word was that QPR was no more than a business venture launched by Briatore and Ecclestone in the year 2007, with total disregard for the history, traditions and values of more than 120 previous years. I'd continued to make a few appearances on BBC London's sports shows and, on one occasion, the presenter – I can't recall who it was – prefaced our chat with a brief clip of Sousa's most recent comments, which included the 'p' word! Of course, that riled me somewhat and, whatever the opening question had been, I kicked off with, 'Well, the first thing I want to stress is that QPR isn't a project. It's a football club.' Sorry, Paulo – just had to get that in!

I suppose there may be fellow journalists, a bit younger than myself, who read this with a certain degree of incredulity. 'What's this guy grumbling about?' they must be thinking. 'Why would you expect to have any kind of one-to-one relationship with the manager (or coach) of a football club?' Because the landscape has altered so dramatically in the last ten years or so, they've had to get used to a process whereby all interaction with the manager comes through formal press conferences. That suits clubs perfectly, of course – it ensures that, by and large, they can control the message. It also involves lumping every section of the media into one basket – TV, radio, agencies, national newspapers, regional newspapers and so on all together, making the assumption that all of them have the same requirements and agenda. It's lazy – and crazy. I've been to press conferences where, as a representative of the local press, you might want to ask about a specific player's new role in the team, or an update on his return from injury. But if it isn't one of the club's 'star names', the bulk of journalists in attendance haven't the slightest interest and may make it clear they think that area of discussion is a waste of time. Nobody's right or wrong – it just highlights the need for some alternative channel of communication and a certain degree of trust between club and journalist. That had always been my *modus operandi* and I can truthfully say I'd never betrayed that trust. As Phil Harris had proved during the time we'd worked together, it was perfectly possible for an arrangement like that to suit everyone.

Throughout my time in local newspapers, I suppose my guiding principle was to try and offer the reader something different. Not necessarily something that was shocking or sensational, just different. Whether that meant new information, or a new angle or voice on an existing story, there seemed little point in simply repeating something that was already in the public domain – why should anyone bother to read it again?

Nowadays press conferences, especially at the top level of football, are all about theatre and spectacle rather than the process of journalists asking questions to find out information. In a sense it's not surprising that the whole set-up is TV-friendly – that, after all, is the source of most of the game's income. At the same time, it does reduce the chances of any meaningful or interesting conversation taking place.

None of this is intended as a specific criticism of Paulo Sousa – or, in fact, QPR. I'm trying to make the point that, from my perspective, it was becoming far harder to do the job with the same degree of satisfaction – leaving aside the wider issues that were starting to cloud my personal, as well as professional, relationship with the club!

In fact, I was impressed by Sousa in that he evidently wasn't content to go along with the players Briatore had foisted on him – and duly sent both Tommasi and Parejo packing within weeks. With that said, it was clear that Gianni had been dusting down his little black book once more – or at least fishing out particular numbers – and at last secured the centre-forward Rangers had been desperate for since the summer in the shape of Heidar Helguson. Despite missing a sitter on his debut at Crystal Palace, Helguson proved a welcome addition to the side and went on to find the net regularly – as well as providing the pretext for some corny headlines on account of his nationality. The Iceman cometh, breaking the ice, frozen out at Bolton ... you get the idea.

However, apart from brief pockets of entertainment such as a 3-2 win against Preston just before Christmas – in which Helguson scored twice – the football was mostly forgettable, certainly by comparison with some of the stuff the Loftus Road crowd had been enjoying earlier in the year. Sousa probably didn't help himself with his apparent reluctance to pair Helguson with Dexter Blackstock – he preferred to operate with one or the other, as a lone target man, which attracted plenty of criticism. Blackstock, in particular, was the kind of striker who functioned more effectively as part of a pair, and personally I would also have liked to see them play together. But it's worth stressing that Blackstock was given plenty of game time under the Portuguese – contrary to some of the nonsense that was spun once the club set about trashing Sousa's reputation a few months later.

It seemed unlikely, though, that Sousa would have made Gary Borrowdale, Coventry's out-of-favour left-back, a top target – or, for that matter, Wayne Routledge, who arrived as soon as the January window opened. Rangers had first tried to sign the former Crystal Palace winger a year earlier and he looked the business right away, scoring once and setting up the second goal in a 2-0 win at Derby.

I'd travelled to Pride Park with David McIntyre and neither of us expected QPR to dominate the game as they did. It was Derby's first home match under a new manager, Nigel Clough, but quite frankly they were outclassed – Rangers could have won by more and, working on the basis that players are more inclined to give interviews after a good performance, we made our way towards the team bus. First up was Lee Cook, who you knew wouldn't refuse to chat – and didn't – but we were a little more wary of approaching Routledge, rumour had it that he wasn't terribly media-friendly. Having plucked up the courage to ask whether he could spare a couple of minutes – always 'a couple of minutes', by the way, which is suitably vague – we were pleasantly surprised by the response: 'Yeah, why not?' Routledge turned out to be a pretty good interviewee and said all the right things – praise for the quality of his team-mates, a play-off place should be the minimum target for Rangers, etc. It was a lesson in how wildly inaccurate a player's reputation can sometimes turn out to be.

That Derby win came at a cost, with Martin Rowlands stretchered off and ruled out for the rest of the season with a torn cruciate ligament, and I felt bad for him, not least because I'd had a dig at him in the paper a few days earlier. As club captain, Rowlands put his name to a column in the matchday programme, and the most recent one had criticised fans for booing the team, saying they 'need to have some sort of reality check'. I felt that seemed a bit rich, given that the owners were constantly boasting about how ambitious they were and telling QPR supporters what a wonderful 'brand' and 'project' they were building. Once again, they were missing the point of football. Fans couldn't care less about any of that corporate guff – they want to be entertained and to see their team winning. Now they were expected to dig deeper into their pockets to watch a series of drab 0-0 draws.

But Briatore was particularly sensitive to the jeers – those who have seen the Four Year Plan won't have forgotten the scene where he demanded the names of those who were booing him! Mind you, even that wasn't quite as jaw-dropping as the line he delivered in response to criticism at the Loftus Road entrance one matchday: 'I own this club and I own you too.'

Despite Briatore's baleful presence, it wasn't all bad and I made a conscious effort to try and ensure we balanced the newspaper coverage with positive news rather than swamping it in complete cynicism. Rangers' youngsters had enjoyed a rare run to the latter stages of the FA Youth Cup and landed a high-profile tie against Newcastle, so we ran a feature ahead of the game with Steve Brown, who was in charge of the Centre of Excellence at the time. For me, it seemed a good opportunity to showcase the club's youth set-up and push for a return to the Academy status they'd had to surrender after tumbling into administration. Now, the owners certainly had the money to fund the necessary upgrade. Sadly, they didn't have the slightest interest in doing so.

I watched the youth team put up a decent performance at Loftus Road, although Newcastle triumphed 3-1. Needless to say, the owners were conspicuous by their absence – they really didn't make any pretence at being interested in anything beyond first-team level. That also applied to the launch of the QPR Community Trust, which took place a few weeks later at the Houses of Parliament. For once, the glamorous venue was nothing to do with Briatore's PR wonks – the event was hosted by Lord Burns, a QPR fan who had been a non-executive director during Chris Wright's chairmanship. Needless to say, Briatore and Ecclestone were conspicuous by their absence – but Amit was there, giving the Community scheme his full backing and also agreeing to become chair of trustees.

Even if it meant digging out a shirt and tie for the Westminster reception, I was more than happy to publicise the excellent work that Andy Evans – who seems to have been running the QPR Community department forever! – and his team were doing. He and Amit were both happy to give interviews on the night and, inevitably, I was keen to get their views on whether the Trust's work could also help draw local talent to QPR and eventually into the first team. Not too long ago, that kind of thing had happened on a fairly regular basis – as I pointed out, Rangers had two west London boys, Kevin Gallen and Danny Dichio, leading the line in the Premier League at one time.

Amit's response to my question was, 'It would be like swimming in the sea and finding a lost diamond!' Nice quote and, while I knew from the way he'd said it the thought the chance of unearthing local talent might be remote, I wanted to present Amit's comment as something he at least felt was desirable.

Most of Rangers' first-team squad also attended the launch and, in keeping with the theme of my question to Amit, I asked to interview Angelo Balanta. He'd been spotted playing for a Sunday League side in Fulham and was now on the fringes of the first team, so he seemed a good candidate to give his views on the issue at hand. Interestingly, Angelo spoke at length about how Paulo Sousa had encouraged him and assured him he'd be given opportunities to play, especially in his favoured formation that included two wide men. It was good to hear evidence that the coach valued young talent, even if the club's owners didn't.

The bad news for Balanta's prospects of regular football was that Sousa's days at QPR were already numbered. I travelled up to the game at Barnsley and bumped into Gianni on the way into Oakwell. Although the ex-chairman didn't welcome my phone calls any more, he was still perfectly friendly when our paths happened to cross and we exchanged greetings. 'I suppose he's playing one up front again today?' Gianni asked. The line-ups hadn't been announced yet, so I didn't know, but if the implication was that Helguson and Blackstock should play together I certainly couldn't disagree. We discussed it briefly before Gianni came out with, 'He's shit. He's going soon.'

I wasn't overly surprised by that remark, given the way QPR had operated when Gianni was in charge as well as since. Now it was just a case of whether the club would bother finding a pretext to give Sousa his cards, or sack him without explanation as they'd done with Dowie. Ironically, the coach sprang a tactical surprise for that game at Oakwell, leaving out Gavin Mahon and including both his main strikers in a 4-4-2 formation – yet Rangers still went down to a 2-1 defeat. Hopes of a top-six finish seemed to be disappearing fast after another loss, at home to Norwich a few days later, and I headlined the back page 'Play-off … or pay-off?' It was obviously going to be one or the other.

In the end, Blackstock was the chosen vehicle for Sousa's downfall. I rang the striker before Rangers' trip to Southampton – mainly to do a run of the mill 'player returns to former club' story, but also to ask about reports that he had stalled on signing a new three-year contract with QPR. Blackstock was quite clear about the situation, telling me, 'I've got less than 18 months remaining on my present contract and, until I'm offered another one, I can't sign it. Nothing's been said about it at the moment.'

Two weeks later, Blackstock arrived at Harlington to be informed by Paladini that he was being sent on loan to Nottingham Forest for the rest of the season. He'd known nothing about the move and nor, it transpired, had the coach. Sousa admitted as such when he spoke to the press after QPR's next game, a 0-0 draw against Crystal Palace that was livelier than the scoreline might suggest. He was duly dismissed a few days later for what the club claimed was 'divulging confidential information' and therefore a breach of his contract.

To put the Blackstock decision into some kind of context, his departure came after back-to-back home victories against Swansea and Bristol City had just about kept Rangers in with a glimmer of a play-off place. His return of 12 goals during the season was by far the highest in the squad. Injuries to Helguson and Patrick Agyemang meant Sousa was left with only one frontline option – teenager Samuel Di Carmine, who had scored a few goals, but certainly wasn't up to leading the attack on his own. It wasn't all that hard to work out the identity of the footballing genius who took the decision to put the block on talks of a new contract and then offload Blackstock altogether.

In one sense, you had to laugh. At least that was how I felt when a swish piece of marketing literature from QPR dropped onto my doorstep in that same week, offering fans a payment scheme for their 2009-10 season tickets. Featuring a cover image of – guess who? Dexter Blackstock!

The reason that leaflet came my way is that I'd retained my club membership until that point. Even after my media work negated the reasons for buying a season ticket, I continued to be a QPR member – it was a way of affirming my connection to the club, I suppose, and it also increased your chances of helping friends and relatives to obtain tickets for a potential play-off or cup final (a long shot, perhaps). After the events of that season, I'd reluctantly decided that I wouldn't be renewing membership any longer. In any walk of life, being a member of a club must indicate some level of pride in what that club stands for. I was finding it difficult to identify with what QPR now appeared to stand for – arrogance and greed, an attitude of short-termism and total disregard for the club's traditions.

The Blackstock leaflet made it clear that they were taking their fanbase for fools. So I had no compunction about the back-page comment I wrote that week, alongside a reproduction of the ill-timed cover:

*The message couldn't be clearer: stump up your cash right now if you want to watch QPR's top goalscorer in action next season!*

*That's him. Dexter Blackstock – Rangers' poster boy, the face of the club's future … and on loan to a club in the Championship relegation zone.*

*You could have been forgiven for thinking it was an early April Fool's joke. Sadly, it was very much in keeping with the absurd, asinine way QPR conduct their football business these days.*

*But it will be fascinating to see what effect the astonishing decision to offload Blackstock to Nottingham Forest has on Rangers fans pondering whether or not to renew their season tickets.*

*Some fans will be wondering why this supposedly 'ambitious' club are so keen to part with a player who has hit the net more than twice as often as anyone else this season.*

*Or why the club – following two good home wins that kept the door to the play-offs fractionally ajar – appear to be slamming it shut by sending out such a negative message.*

*Or why on earth supporters should part with more hard-earned cash so that the board can squander it on ridiculous signings like Daniel Parejo, Damiano Tommasi and Gary Borrowdale all over again.*

You never quite know how these kind of things will go down, but I was pleasantly surprised by the reaction from my colleague Lorraine King, who was the paper's chief reporter at the time. Lorraine wasn't the world's most enthusiastic football follower – although she had been to Loftus Road once – but she greeted me with a hug after reading that back page! Not something that happened too often, unless it had been a long evening in the pub …

In all seriousness, Lorraine – who was absolutely superb at reporting on the Brent area, somewhere she knew like the back of her hand – recognised the point I was trying to put across, namely that the QPR fans were being taken for a ride. At the same time, I was aware that I was now beginning to stray into dangerous territory. It was one thing to be critical of the owners, trying to expose the deep flaws in their chaotic running of the club. Questioning whether fans should continue to give the club financial support could be seen as another matter altogether. Over the next year, I'd find myself drifting closer and closer to that red line and eventually across it.

# 10

# TIME TO GO, FLAVIO

### (September 2009)

QPR never actually banned me from the club. It was more subtle than that – and I have to concede, they took a shrewd approach. Plenty of clubs have banned specific journalists or publications in recent years and it almost always backfires. The club are exposed as heavy-handed and overreacting to criticism, while the subject of the ban picks up greater publicity and gets to play the role of heroic martyr, unjustly treated for speaking out. QPR never told me I would be refused entry to Loftus Road or the training ground – however, it was made clear that they would not co-operate with me, mainly in terms of making members of staff available for interview. It was an open-ended sanction, imposed in the autumn of 2009 and to be reviewed, I was told, as and when the club 'saw more evidence of positive reporting'.

Paul Morrissey was the man who delivered that message – and I mean this nicely when I say he was the perfect man to do it! Paul doesn't have an aggressive manner, he always comes across as the epitome of calm and reasonable, to the extent that the other person begins to wonder whether they're being unreasonable by disagreeing. We had a measured discussion, no argument whatsoever and, if that represented a falling out, I always felt it was purely a professional, not a personal one. I remember Paul saying, 'You've made it fairly clear what you think of the new QPR, Ben,' and I couldn't disagree with him. He and Ian Taylor were in the unenviable position of having to promote and defend 'the new QPR', while someone like me was repeatedly attacking it. I know from subsequent conversations with both Paul and Ian that they would have preferred to handle the situation in a different way, but ultimately they didn't make the decisions. Heavy hints were dropped from the boardroom to the effect that the club shouldn't be engaging with a journalist who took what they considered such a consistently negative stance.

I wouldn't deny that, during the six months leading up to the 'semi-ban', if I can call it that, I'd become ever more disillusioned and the paper's coverage of QPR may have reflected that. At the same time, I was encouraged by the knowledge that there were numerous other Rangers supporters who shared my views.

That was something Paul himself couldn't fail to be aware of – especially after he was booed at the home game against Sheffield Wednesday that followed Paulo Sousa's sacking! Paul was required to stand on the pitch and read out the club statement about the former coach ahead of kick-off – which, unsurprisingly, didn't go down at all well with the crowd as it was an undignified, thinly-veiled attack on Sousa. The statement stressed how few games Sousa had won during his time at QPR – and, suddenly, the 3-0 defeat at Vicarage Road had been slapped back on his record!

The match itself, with Gareth back in temporary charge, was actually a rare thriller as QPR went 2-0 down, prompting fans to sing the name of their leading scorer – who, as already mentioned, was now wearing a Nottingham Forest shirt. Instead, though, Rowan Vine made his return from injury and began the fightback as Rangers ended up winning 3-2. Although there was nothing left to play for that season, I made sure I got myself along to the handful of fixtures that remained. The first of those was away to champions-elect Wolves – a fairly predictable one in that QPR always seemed to find themselves cast as a guest at someone else's promotion celebrations. That was the basic theme I focused on – Wolves, at the time, were a shining example of how sticking with a manager, allowing him to build a promotion-winning team over a number of years, could bear fruit. Mick McCarthy's side were going up as deserved champions, while Rangers – for all Briatore's posturing – had changed manager three times and were destined to finish in mid-table. Yet I doubted that would prompt the owners into a change of tone over the summer – and, sure enough, it didn't.

I spoke to Gavin Mahon after the final home game, a dull 0-0 draw against Plymouth, but he certainly wasn't buying into the idea that the team's failure to make the top six could be put down to a lack of continuity in the dugout. He said, 'You could put anyone in charge of this team. Whatever 11 we put on the pitch should be good enough to get a result but at times we haven't performed – whoever's been in charge, we've let them down.' Mahon, who had taken over as captain after Martin Rowlands' injury, always came across as a good talker and, in anything resembling normal circumstances, I'd probably have approached him as a potential columnist.

The issue of the column was one I'd been pondering for some time. Richard Langley had taken it on during the second half of the season and, as I mentioned earlier, brought a really fresh approach to the whole concept. Around that time, Langers had seen his playing career stalled somewhat due to injuries and he was starting to look at other options, including the media – so having him write a column for the local papers really suited everyone. I met him at Brian Melzack's office one afternoon to talk the idea over and, from my point of view, it worked like a dream. Langers would sometimes speak to other ex-QPR players to get their opinions on the club, as well as inviting fans to submit questions relating to his career and football in general. In my unbiased opinion, his answers made good reading – along with the fact that, being on the outside, he could be honest and objective when it came to assessing the ongoing issues at Loftus Road.

However, Langers also made it clear that he hadn't yet hung up his boots – he had a number of trials lined up that summer and, obviously, if one of those worked out he wouldn't really be able to continue giving unfettered opinions on a rival club. However, the idea of a former player doing a regular column was a good one – my colleague who covered Arsenal did just that with Nigel Winterburn and I was pleased that one of my successors, Sean Gallagher, later persuaded Kevin Gallen to pick up the baton on QPR.

For the time being, we went along a different route. I'd done a Q&A for Adam Boxer, who ran the Vital QPR website at that time, and asked him if he'd be interested in contributing a fans' column, initially as an experimental one-off at the end of the season. Quite apart from anything else, I thought it wouldn't be a bad idea to help get more supporters' opinions out there as the board were by that stage – with the exception of Amit – refusing to engage with the concerns of the fanbase. Having said that, I made it clear to Adam he was free to take whatever stance he chose. As he and most others knew by then, I had firmly held views of my own, but it wasn't my place to set up a one-man ministry of censorship!

Adam sent me a really good, descriptive reflection on the season just gone and we turned it into a regular feature once 2009-10 kicked off, rotating among a pool of four or five writers. Like all columns, it needed a title, so I resurrected 'Beat around the Bush', which Dave Evans had used some years earlier when he'd been sports editor. I suppose I was fast running out of original ideas – even 'On the Ball with Langers' had been a case of reaching fairly deep into the creative well!

Having praised Paul Morrissey's cool head, the closest I ever got to seeing him lose it came during Rangers' final game of that season, at Preston. The cause? Well, it was one of my media colleagues – a radio reporter who I'll call Jim. Because that isn't his name. But I'd be willing to bet most journalists who have ever encountered him will know who I'm talking about.

Jim's general strategy is to approach one or two journalists who report on the away team before kick-off and try to glean some information. Nothing wrong with making use of local knowledge, most of us do exactly the same. But I'd like to think most of us also remember some of that information next time we visit – Jim rarely seems to. So you can easily end up having basically the same conversation with him every few months. One of the phrases he frequently employs is, 'Now, I've done my research' … before going on to prove beyond doubt that he hasn't. Another curious, yet regular, line of enquiry revolves around the appropriate nickname for the away side – in this case, 'Are they Rangers, or the Rs?'

'Well, either's fine,' I remember replying, to which Jim wanted to know, 'But which is better?'

Another of Jim's obsessions is to check exactly where the visiting manager will be available to give post-match interviews. Paul, who was flying solo for the QPR media department that day, had a million and one things to do before kick-off and really could have done without Jim's persistent questioning. 'Now, will Gareth Ainsworth be able to speak after the game?' 'Yes, I'll bring him up here.' 'Right, he'll definitely be coming up here?' 'Yes.' 'You're quite sure of that?' 'I've already told you he will.' 'Only, I do need to speak to him. So you'll bring him in here?' 'YES!'

Poor old Jim. He also has an unfortunate tendency to experience technical mishaps and, a few years later, confounded Paul further by asking if he could get the QPR manager to do the interview again as his recording equipment had failed!

On this occasion, fortunately, Jim did get his interview with Gareth and it followed a strong Rangers performance as they pushed Preston – who needed a win to reach the play-offs – right to the end before going down 2-1. Despite that, it was hard to disguise the fact that the team had made little progress over the past year and I wrote a summary of the season that was a tad more satirical than Adam's. The comparison I made related to the final series of *Blackadder*, set during the First World War – an episode where the deranged General Melchett, played by Stephen Fry, justifies the casualty list by noting that his troops have recaptured 17 square feet of land. In similar fashion, QPR gave the impression that they felt an extra three points, compared with the previous season's tally, was clear proof that they were on the right track!

OK, maybe it was a mischievous comparison – maybe some would see it as juvenile. What I'd say in response is that QPR were being run by people who had forfeited any right to be taken seriously. They were alienating the supporters and turning the club into a laughing stock – so ridicule seemed entirely appropriate. In fact, with hindsight I should have spent some time photoshopping Briatore's face onto that of the equally comical General Melchett.

Until that year, I'd always been concerned about trying to make sure we kept our coverage of QPR ticking over during the close season. But I was aware the enthusiasm was beginning to drain on my part and, subconsciously, I was looking elsewhere, not just to fill space in the paper but also to regain that sense of enjoyment I'd previously found through reporting on Rangers. Covering James DeGale's professional career as it began to gather pace, along with some of the other up-and-coming boxers in the area, was one such avenue. In a greater way, so was my gradual reconnection with another sporting love – Middlesex cricket. I'd followed the county side keenly as a kid and drifted away a bit, but changes of personnel around this time in the Archant sports department provided an opening for me to take over Middlesex coverage for all our titles in North and West London. That summer, I started attending more and more matches at Lord's, as well as Southgate and Uxbridge, I got to know more of the county's players and staff and enjoyed writing about them. I suppose, if I try to apply a bit of self-analysis, Middlesex filled a psychological gap – it was somewhere I felt at home, maybe welcome or valued to some extent. That feeling was beginning to slip away at QPR. Going to Loftus Road seemed like coming home to find someone else had bought the place, redecorated your lounge overnight and now you could like it or lump it.

For a while that summer, I was left wondering whether my time on *the Times* series (so to speak) might be up in any case. The implications of the financial crash were being well and truly felt in regional newspapers, along with most other businesses, and that inevitably translated into cutbacks. Initially the Archant line was that they preferred to 'lose buildings instead of people', closing down many of their London offices and moving the staff into two hubs at Ilford and Swiss Cottage. What later became clear was that they'd actually meant 'buildings as well as people'.

Getting down to specifics, they announced that the three 'senior' sports staff on the North and West London titles – Pat Mooney, Paul Chronnell and myself – would be reduced to two. This was my first experience of the redundancy process and, without stating the obvious, it wasn't nice – because there are no winners in those situations. In simple terms, you either depart or you stay and take on more work for the same money. It's a very uncomfortable feeling to be forced, in effect, into competition with colleagues who you like and respect. I think they'd lined up some rather ludicrous 'tests' for us, basically to check whether we could actually do the job they were already paying us for – but in the end those weren't necessary. I took a call from Pat, inviting me to join him in the Swiss Cottage pub, where he informed me of his decision to pack it in, take the pay-off and spend more time on the golf course. So that was that, I stayed on and did my best to put the distraction behind me.

Once again, of course, the immediate issue to be settled at QPR that summer was the identity of the next managerial victim. Frankly, it was largely a case of guesswork when it came to speculating about the new boss because even Gianni, it appeared, was keeping his cards relatively close to his chest on this one. My limited understanding of the situation was that the club had eventually decided to offer the job to former Watford boss Aidy Boothroyd, although Jim Magilton was also in the frame, along with an improbable comeback for Gigi de Canio. Some years later, Boothroyd revealed in a national newspaper interview that he'd been under the impression he'd landed a job at a Championship club, only to experience a rude awakening when he saw they'd appointed somebody else. While he didn't name QPR specifically, joining up the dots wasn't too difficult a task.

Annoyingly, the club chose a Wednesday afternoon to confirm Magilton's arrival – an hour or two after the paper had gone to print. I'd illustrated the back page with a silhouette of a man wearing a long coat, to underline how successfully QPR had kept the new manager's identity under wraps, while mentioning the names of the three leading candidates. Maybe not ideal, but I don't think it mattered too much in the scheme of things.

Slightly to my surprise, I was allowed to speak to Ali Russell a few days after the manager's appointment and wrote what the club must surely have seen as a positive story! It was no secret that almost half of Rangers' season ticket holders had been slow to get their renewals in – maybe, like me, they had been less than impressed by that Blackstock leaflet. Russell's line was that, with the uncertainty about the manager's position now ended, fans would be feeling reassured and encouraged to fork out for next season. I'd also hoped there might be an opportunity to meet Magilton in the near future and put that to Ian Taylor, who said he'd try to arrange something – although it took more than a month! Perhaps the new boss was on an extended holiday, I don't know. So in the short term, I gave Steve Lomas a ring – he'd played alongside Magilton in the Northern Ireland midfield for several years and was happy to talk up the new manager's credentials. At the same time, he stressed the point, 'It's time for someone to get in there and be given at least a couple of years.' Fat chance.

Meanwhile, I took myself off to the London Masters six-a-side tournament at Wembley Arena. The competition was a lot of fun – it's always interesting to see which ex-pros have kept in shape and which have let themselves go since retirement! In my view, it also seemed a great opportunity to catch up with some of the former QPR players and get their opinions on current issues. Strangely, there were never very many journalists in attendance at these events, which meant picking up interviews all to yourself was straightforward. Even better, it was a chance to see a QPR team compete on an equal footing with the capital's Premier League clubs – and on this occasion actually win the trophy too. Danny Maddix, who was the Rangers captain on the night, said afterwards, 'That's the first time I've won anything for QPR!'

As well as speaking to Danny, I also interviewed Andy Sinton and Bradley Allen. Bradley, who I used to see on the circuit quite frequently in his role as an analyst for BBC London, spoke about how he'd like to see Rangers bring in a striker who could lead the line as Les Ferdinand had in his day. Andy, who was managing in non-league at the time, was happy to talk about the wingers and so on. It gave me a stack of decent material to spread over the next few weeks, while QPR's present-day squad got down to the business of pre-season.

Heading down to Aldershot for the first of Rangers' friendlies, I was surprised to see the name Dexter Blackstock on the team sheet. Somehow he'd ended up back at QPR while they negotiated with Nottingham Forest over a permanent transfer and played the second half, scoring the final goal in a 4-0 win. Bizarrely, asking Magilton about the striker's future at the club afterwards took me back to that conversation with Iain Dowie a year ago, when Lee Camp had been transfer-listed against his wishes.

This time, Dowie's successor said, 'As I see it, Dexter's a QPR player and you haven't heard anything from me to reverse that situation.' Magilton's carefully worded response indicated to me that he'd gone into the job with his eyes firmly open – he knew perfectly well how the club operated and was making it fairly plain that when Blackstock's move eventually went through it would be none of his doing. The reality, of course, was that QPR's transfer policy was conducted by the same man it had been for years – Gianni, at Briatore's bidding – and so the same scattergun approach continued. Adel Taarabt, who had briefly arrived on loan from Tottenham the previous season, rejoined on a longer loan – although Magilton already had numerous creative options. Italian striker Alessandro Pellicori somehow landed himself a contract despite looking somewhat unimpressive during pre-season – and the club then brought in another forward, Arsenal's Jay Simpson on loan, a few weeks later. Meanwhile, Rangers went into the new season with just one senior goalkeeper, having failed to agree terms with Magilton's former Ipswich team-mate Andy Marshall, and Gary Borrowdale as their only recognised left-back.

Perhaps the most extraordinary move of the lot was Ben Watson. Like Wayne Routledge, he was among the players Dowie had hoped to bring in from his promotion-winning Palace side – and ended up at Loftus Road anyway, long after Dowie had cleared his desk. But it seemed odd to prioritise signing a virtual clone of Martin Rowlands when the captain was returning to fitness. Oh, and they'd also just bought another central midfielder from Argentina named Alejandro Faurlin – whose transfer was inaccurately billed as a club record at the time, but would later come under scrutiny for a very different reason.

Magilton made a comparison with Steven Gerrard and Frank Lampard when I asked him to comment on Watson's arrival, saying, 'They can play as a pair, most certainly. I think good players rebound off good players.' A fair answer, I suppose, but perhaps skating over the widely held consensus that Gerrard and Lampard tended to perform better in an England shirt without the other's presence!

I really liked Magilton's number two, John Gorman. Enormously experienced in the game, much of it as sidekick to Glenn Hoddle, he was shrewd and easy to talk to. I spoke to him about Rangers' prospects ahead of the new season and he had plenty to say about the squad and football in general. Incessant transfer speculation, for instance, was something Gorman found exasperating. 'I wish people would stop asking if we're going to buy players,' he told me. 'Fans all over the country are almost forcing managers to go and buy players, but what does it do? It takes players time to settle in together.'

I couldn't have agreed with him more. Gorman, I felt, was more about developing players than buying them, and that was one reason I alerted him to the fact that Wealdstone, only a few miles down the road, were keen to establish a system of borrowing youngsters from nearby Championship clubs to give them first-team experience. The non-league side already had very strong links with Watford in that regard, but I was aware they were also looking to set up some kind of relationship with QPR.

Gorman was immediately interested when I mentioned it. 'That could be just what we need for Elvijs,' he said, referring to Rangers' young Latvian goalkeeper. 'I'll talk to the boss.' As far as I'm aware, nothing came of that idea – I think the club had another non-league loan in mind for him – but it was good to see Gorman's reaction. I believe Wealdstone's manager, Gordon Bartlett, did try and arrange a meeting with QPR later that season, but got nowhere – and of course, by then, Gorman and Magilton were long gone. In fact, when I thanked the assistant manager for his time and got up to leave, Gorman revealed his prescient streak by replying, 'Come in for another chat around Christmas-time if you like – assuming we're still here, that is!'

I used some of Gorman's comments in our final edition before the Championship season got under way, but it'd be a distortion of the truth to describe it as a new season supplement of any kind. A year earlier, we'd put together a 12-page pull-out, whereas the 2009 version was a double-page spread within the sports section. Realistically, the economic climate made it far harder for the sales team to bring in the volume of advertising that would be needed in any case. And editorially? Being brutally honest, I didn't have the same level of motivation any more. There seemed little point in running in-depth interviews with new signings who you knew, within a matter of months, would probably be replaced by more of the same.

However, I did use the available space to include a sizeable piece with Steve Gallen, who had just been promoted to youth development manager, with Birch rejoining the club as his assistant. Like his brothers, Steve represented 'my' QPR

– he was a local boy, he understood the importance of community and showing young players a pathway to the first team and he made it clear he was determined to push that cause as much as possible.

Another club stalwart I made a point of seeking out during pre-season was our one-time columnist. After his two spells as caretaker boss, Gareth now found himself reduced to the ranks again, which can't have been an easy situation, and he admitted that unless he could force his way into Magilton's side it'd be time to move on. 'Last year was a very confusing situation for everybody and going into management wasn't my ideal choice,' he told me. 'In hindsight, maybe it was a bit early for me. I've got plenty more running and crossing balls to do until people tell me I can't do it any more.'

I'm sure Gareth was realistic enough to know that his chances of getting much game time under Magilton were slim and he continued to twiddle his thumbs even though Rangers made an uncertain start to the season. They succeeded in winning only one of their first six league games, although it'd be equally accurate to say they only lost once – a good example of how statistics can usually be manipulated to suit your narrative. The difficulty of scoring goals seemed to have lingered from the previous season, with Helguson struggling badly and eventually returning to Watford on loan, Simpson still finding his feet and Pellicori – to nobody's great surprise – not looking up to the standard required. In spite of the way the board tended to operate, I can't say I ever had the impression Magilton was under pressure from them, and nor should he have been. He'd been landed with a surfeit of players who operated in that undefined area between midfield and attack and was doing his best to shoehorn them all into a system, but you could see people were literally getting in each other's way on the field at times. Apart from anything else, Magilton had managed to steer Rangers beyond the second round of the Carling Cup again! Anything resembling a cup run should always bring brownie points for a QPR manager – not that it had worked that way for Dowie the previous year – but, once again, Rangers had landed an eye-catching third-round tie with another trip to Stamford Bridge.

I'd begun to take a more sparing approach towards away games, looking to reduce expenses and not because of general disillusionment with the club, and that meant I'd missed the first league win of the season, at Scunthorpe. I was also absent from the second, a 2-0 victory against Cardiff which my stand-in assured me had been Rangers' most impressive performance so far. But there was no way

I'd miss out on another clash with Chelsea. It's incredible how the prospect of a game against your local rivals – and for a QPR fan growing up when I did, they genuinely were our closest rivals – can top up your enthusiasm levels, no matter what else is going on.

The obvious angle to preview the Chelsea tie was a look back at QPR's most recent victory at the Bridge – the quarter-final of the same competition back in 1986. I rang Alan McDonald, who had scored the first goal in that 2-0 win and enjoyed reminiscing with him about that header, Michael Robinson scoring the second from the halfway line and, as Macca put it, the pleasure of being able to 'ram Mr Bates's comments back down his throat'. This was the era when Ken Bates, the Chelsea chairman, loved to sound off in their match programme and, after drawing 1-1 on the artificial pitch at Loftus Road, he'd confidently proclaimed that QPR wouldn't pose his side too many problems on grass. Interviewing Macca ahead of the game was more than an exercise in self-indulgence – I honestly felt it was important to stress how much taking on Chelsea meant to Rangers supporters, something that tended to escape the notice of most national media. A couple of years later, when the teams finally met again in the Premier League, some of the Chelsea players looked visibly shocked and unsettled by the hostility of the Loftus Road crowd – none would have realised the significance that this derby once held.

Sadly, the outcome was the same as it had been for the FA Cup tie in 2008, with Salomon Kalou scoring the only goal to send Chelsea through. But, again, Rangers hadn't disgraced themselves and the performance maintained the general upturn that would gather pace through the autumn.

In that same week, I lit the fuse that finally made the QPR hierarchy explode at me. Briatore had hit the headlines over his role in what became known as Formula 1's 'Crashgate' affair, when it transpired that he had told Renault driver Nelson Piquet Jr to crash deliberately at the Singapore Grand Prix and thereby improve team-mate Fernando Alonso's chances of victory. The fall-out left Briatore disgraced, forced his resignation as Renault team director and he was banned from Formula 1 entirely, although that decision was later overturned in court and he reached a settlement with the sport's governing body.

I'd never cast myself as anything approaching an expert when it came to motorsport, but at the time it seemed crystal clear that morally – if not legally – a person with those stains on his character could not be seen as suitable to run a football club. So I felt it was justifiable to publicly say Briatore should leave QPR. I outlined all the reasons why his tenure had been a disaster for the club – the interference in team affairs, the constant changes of manager and players, the steep ticket prices, the poor treatment of club stalwarts, the fallacy that QPR couldn't have survived without him … and so on. All things I'd spoken out about in the past. I tried to make it hard-hitting and headlined the piece 'Time to go, Flavio', accompanied by a large red no-smoking sign on top of Briatore's face. I invited readers to get in touch and give their thoughts on the QPR owner. None of it would have been well received at Loftus Road, I'm sure. But, as I subsequently learned, basically it was the final sentence that came to be viewed as the final straw.

*It may fall to his fellow board members to tell Briatore his time is up. But the fans can play a part by joining our campaign, by voicing their disapproval at matches, or even staying away from matches altogether.*

I can see why that line, in many people's eyes, would seem far too strong. Essentially, I was suggesting supporters should stop supporting their club while Briatore remained in charge, and I knew I could expect plenty of brickbats as well as bouquets. However, it reflected my own feelings as a QPR fan at the time.

After that, it didn't come as a complete surprise when I turned up to the home game against Barnsley a couple of days later to be greeted by Paul Morrissey with the words, 'Ben, could I have a word with you outside, please?'

# 11

# DON'T WASTE OUR TIME ON THIS RUBBISH

### (December 2009)

It was just my luck, I suppose, when QPR served up their biggest goal-fest of the season in the aftermath of my conversation with Paul Morrissey. With Akos Buzsaky in full flow, Rangers put five past Barnsley after the visitors had threatened a comeback at 3-2 and it all made for entertaining viewing. I wasn't really able to fully appreciate the game, though, reflecting on the implications of the club's non-co-operation policy and wondering how severely it would restrict my work. It was also a moment to take stock and acknowledge just how drastically my relationship with QPR had changed. Just two years earlier, I'd been close enough – and trusted sufficiently – to speak at Ray Jones's memorial service. I felt as if I was a part of the club, basically. Now, as Paul had just outlined, I was persona non grata.

In professional and practical terms, it turned out to make far less difference than you might have expected. For starters, I had quite a few 'timeless' quotes up my sleeve – material from recent interviews that hadn't made the cut due to a lack of space, but could be used later on, as and when appropriate. An immediate example were some comments from Buzsaky about which position he preferred to play in – those could now form the basis of a story following his performance against Barnsley. But over the coming months I also realised there wasn't a great deal to stop me ringing a player up if I already had his number in my contacts book – and, equally, I could still approach them after matches. It just meant hanging around near the car park rather than sitting down in the press room! Most of the players knew me by sight, some by name, and I seriously doubted

Ian and Paul would have gone to the trouble of circulating a formal directive that I was to be blanked. On top of that, I'd come to realise that most footballers may recognise individuals among the media, but rarely remember which particular outlet they write or broadcast for. Giving one interview is viewed much the same as giving another, to the extent that some don't even distinguish between the club's own in-house media and the rest. Some years later, I asked Alex Oxlade-Chamberlain if he had the proverbial 'few minutes' after a game, to which he replied, 'Sorry, I did an interview this morning!' Whether it had been for his club's website, official magazine or YouTube channel was irrelevant – the Ox clearly felt he'd discharged his media duties for the day. The growth of Twitter has also helped to accentuate that confusion, I think – often a journalist whose name is associated with a particular club becomes a bigger brand (to borrow some Briatore terminology) than the name of their newspaper, website or radio station.

I spent a lot of time over the next week sifting through the emails I'd received in response to my anti-Briatore comments – far more, it must be said, than at any other time I'd invited feedback. I even received one from a guy I hadn't heard from since school! I did find it genuinely interesting that the feelings of Rangers fans were clearly so diverse – some said what I'd written had been 'fantastic' and 'spot on', while others viewed it as 'stupidly counter-productive' and told me I ought to show Briatore more respect. One or two, to be honest, were openly abusive – but they tended to calm down a bit after further reflection. It was also clear that, while many of my correspondents were every bit as disillusioned with Briatore's regime as I was, they felt the suggestion of boycotting the club was a step too far. I filled half a page with a cross-section of fans' comments – having obtained their consent, of course – and my favourite phrase undoubtedly came from one who declared, 'I'd choose financial bankruptcy over moral bankruptcy any day.' Nicely put.

This kind of stuff did tend to get picked up on fans' internet message boards, of course, but it wasn't something I paid a great deal of attention to unless someone else – usually David McIntyre – alerted me to a mention on a particular site. I remember someone posting that I had an axe to grind because I'd previously been 'employed by Gianni' to do the commentary, but I didn't really want to get involved in all that. For the record, as I've already made clear, the commentary gig had been something I did for nothing in any case.

Meanwhile, as long as there were still ways of maintaining our QPR coverage, I was keen to make use of distractions. The cricket season had just finished, unfortunately, but it was very much the right time of year to get involved with our local non-league sides' prospects in the qualifying rounds of the FA Cup. I'd always loved those occasions, when a team well below Football League level could make it through to the first round and potentially overcome the pros – well, apart from the infamous Vauxhall Motors episode in 2002, when QPR had taken on the role of victims!

Picking a favourite among the non-league teams you report on doesn't seem right – maybe it's a bit like a parent being asked to name their favourite child! You surely want them all to do well because, apart from anything else, it makes better reading. But I will admit that, as far as I had a favourite, it was Wealdstone. Perhaps because the club's recent history was so fascinating – they'd gone from non-league double winners to being homeless and dropping down several divisions in less than a decade. But also because, despite that, they'd retained a loyal, sizeable fanbase and had the potential to grow again, especially having moved to a new ground in Ruislip and begun smartening it up. Most of the people involved in running Wealdstone were quite media-savvy as well, and that helped to make it a good place to go and report on a match.

Having watched the Stones crush Lewes, I also went to their tie in the next round, away to Aylesbury FC, and persuaded Dave Brennan to come along too and take some photographs. That probably wouldn't have been our chosen destination a year earlier, for the reason that Rangers were in action at Derby on the same day. But purely in terms of filling space in the paper, I knew a trip to Aylesbury was likely to yield more than pitching up at Pride Park. In another sense, it was a shame to miss seeing Magilton's team really hit their stride as they came from two down to beat Derby 4-2 – having also put four past Preston and Reading within the previous week.

However, I was also delighted to see Wealdstone, who had also recovered a two-goal deficit to win 4-2, gain their reward in the FA Cup first-round draw – a home tie against Rotherham. Difficult, but not completely impossible, and the game turned out to be a cracker, with a full house roaring Wealdstone on as the league side hung on at the end to squeeze through 3-2. But the cup run had been enormously enjoyable to witness and I'd also found it a relief to know the previews, reports and features could command space near the back of the sports section, rather than feeling the pressure to come up with QPR material all the time. In fact, I think our Rangers coverage was shunted further back into the paper during those few weeks than at any other time.

But, with that said, I was always on the lookout for stories of QPR interest. One afternoon I received a phone call from Paul Lawrence, who was in charge of PE at Copland Community School in Wembley. I knew Paul quite well already – he was one of the main organisers of inter-school football in Brent and had also set up a senior side to help promising Copland players to progress in the game. The Copland youngster he'd rung me about was a bit more than just 'promising', however. His name was Raheem Sterling, he was just coming up to his 15th birthday and had recently made his debut for QPR's reserves.

It wasn't the first time Raheem's name had appeared in our sports section – he'd scored the decisive goal to earn Brent boys' football team a gold medal at the prestigious London Youth Games earlier in the year. Quite rightly, though, Paul was keen to showcase the fact Copland had produced a really exciting talent – and that someone like Raheem could be a great role model for other youngsters in the area. He invited me to come along and interview Raheem at the school the following week and, if I remember rightly, the three of us sat on a bench and just chatted about football – Raheem's experiences so far, his prospects at QPR and his ambitions in general.

Raheem spoke highly of Steve Gallen and Gareth Ainsworth, who had been a particular source of encouragement to him – and named Robinho, who was playing for Manchester City at the time, as his favourite player. He also admitted to being a Manchester United fan – somewhat ironic, as he'd go on to make his name with their two greatest rivals! I don't have too many claims to fame, but one I'll proudly hang on to is the honour of being the first journalist to interview Raheem Sterling. I felt satisfied with the end product as well – it was a thoroughly positive story about Raheem, his school, youth football in Brent and, of course, QPR.

Unfortunately, the story appeared to rile rather than please the media department at Loftus Road. On the day we published it, I received a fairly terse email from Ian Taylor asking who had given me permission to speak to Raheem. Was there a problem with the content of the story, I asked? 'No, there isn't,' Ian confirmed. 'But you know our policy – who did you go through to speak to him?'

*Proudly displaying my colours on a trip to Dublin in 1995, the day after watching one of the most gratifying QPR experiences there can ever be – victory against Chelsea.*

*Surveying his new domain... Flavio Briatore oversaw a transformation of QPR, but not in a remotely good way as far as I was concerned.*

*Picture: Dave Brennan*

*Although Clint Hill's arrival from Crystal Palace in 2010 raised a few eyebrows, he proved to be a good value, long-term signing – a rarity for QPR during that period.*

*Hogan Ephraim was one of the players who thrived during Paulo Sousa's brief spell in charge at QPR, likening the Portuguese coach to 'a father figure'.*

*Heidar Helguson's QPR career included several ups and downs, but the Icelander was on the up here with this impressive leap against Barnsley.*

*Jamie Mackie on the charge against Preston. Always popular with the Loftus Road crowd for his whole-hearted approach on the field and a reliable media performer too.*

*Changing managers was a favourite pastime under the Briatore regime, and Jim Magilton lasted six months at QPR. Mind you, that was still longer than most...*

*Most fans love to watch a winger in full flight. Lee Cook ticked that box during his two spells at QPR and he also got to model some of the club's more unusual away kits. Personally I always liked the green and white hoops (left), although I'm not too sure about the yellow and black option as shown against Sheffield United (above)!*

*It's always great when I get the opportunity to go and watch Rangers with my brother, even if I have to wear a cap and shades to ensure people can tell us apart…*

*Normally a very dapper individual, Gigi de Canio is looking a little bedraggled after a wet Tuesday night on the touchline. I think his understanding of English was a lot better than he liked to make out!*

*Somehow Rangers escaped relegation in 2007 with a spirited late rally, celebrated here by the 'Little and Large' combination of Marc Nygaard and Adam Bolder.*

*Rangers fans dressed as clowns for a game against Scunthorpe, highlighting the 'circus' the club had become under Briatore. At least a regular circus wouldn't have charged those prices, mind you!*

*And some fancy dress of my own – a fairly ridiculous hat I wore to the City Ground for QPR's game against Nottingham Forest in 1996. It would be another 15 years before the club returned to the Premier League.*

So that was the issue. It didn't really square with what I'd been told, that the club wanted to see more positive reporting from me, yet here it was both in print and online and they still weren't happy! The implication was totally illogical – what would be the point of seeking their permission to do something, knowing it would be refused?

In any case – as I pointed out to Ian – being under 16, Raheem Sterling was too young to be a contracted QPR player. So, to be blunt, it was none of the club's business if his school had invited me to speak to him.

Meanwhile, Paul Morrissey informed me that Steve Gallen was furious about the story and wanted to know how it had happened. I found that hard to believe – especially as Steve had my phone number and was perfectly capable of telling me that himself. I rang Steve up and said I understood he was absolutely livid with me. Steve was fairly baffled and said, 'What are you talking about? No, I was a bit surprised to read the story, that's all, but I thought it was fine. I don't have a problem with it.'

As I've said before, I regarded any disagreements I had with Ian and Paul as professional rather than personal, and that remains the way I see it today. I was trying to do my job, they were trying to do theirs. I don't know what they were playing at with their reactions to the Raheem Sterling interview, but it's more than likely they were leaned on from above, so to speak.

Incidentally, there weren't too many positive messages to be found on the pitch as autumn advanced into winter – the wheels had suddenly come off for Magilton's side, probably not helped by the regular addition of pointless loan signings. Steven Reid suddenly went into the line-up against Doncaster, having barely played for months, while Tom Heaton's recall from loan by Manchester United left Rangers without a back-up keeper. I travelled to Doncaster with Dave Brennan, who alerted me to the fact that they'd named a young Gaelic footballer from Cricklewood on the bench! It made an interesting alternative angle to the match itself, where Rangers were deservedly beaten 2-0. Warbo was at that game too, and I remember chatting to him not too far from the away dressing-room – where neither of us could help but overhear an enraged Magilton laying into his under-performing side. However, it wasn't long before the relationship between manager and players – or one particular player, at any rate – deteriorated more dramatically.

After watching their team walloped 5-1 by Middlesbrough – Rangers' worst home defeat in 32 years – the supporters had certainly expected to see some fight when the team went to Watford a few days later. As it happened, the fight took place at the end of the 3-1 loss to the Hornets, with Magilton and Akos Buzsaky having what the manager termed 'a difference of opinion'. I was hanging around near the tunnel in the optimistic hope of extracting some comments from one of the QPR players when Buzsaky emerged, still wearing his playing kit, and went to sit by himself in the stand, looking visibly distressed. I did approach Buzsaky, more to see whether he was OK than to request an interview, but he quite reasonably asked to be left alone and that was that. The rest of his team-mates took the best part of an hour to emerge and they'd clearly been instructed not to speak to the media as they made their way back to the bus. However, rumours of the dressing-room confrontation began flying around almost immediately and, while I didn't know with certainty what had happened, one prediction I could safely make was that it would reflect badly on the club.

As it turned out, our main source of reaction came from a former QPR player who was soon to return to the club. Rob Brennan, a freelancer who I knew well – and who would become a full-time Archant colleague a few years later – had spoken to Nigel Quashie and offered to provide us with some copy. Quashie's view was the incident shouldn't be allowed to derail Rangers' season, saying, 'What goes on in the dressing room should be sorted out there. It's nothing strange – just something that happens in football.'

In all honesty, QPR probably handled the situation in the only way they could, with Magilton suspended while they held an internal inquiry and leaving once that had finished. Gorman's loyalty to the manager meant he went too, fulfilling his foreboding that they'd both be gone before Christmas! That meant a familiar problem for Rangers – the need to find a caretaker-manager to take charge of their next game, a televised Monday night trip to West Brom – and this time they were unable to turn to Gareth. He'd signed for Wycombe on loan a few weeks earlier, signalling the end of his distinguished Loftus Road career, although he did at least get the chance to come back and say his farewell when the move became permanent in January. Instead, the wheel of fortune settled on Steve Gallen and Birch, who were asked to lead the team to The Hawthorns – and were ten seconds away from ending up with a 100 per cent win record! West Brom's late equaliser meant a 2-2 draw, but it was nice to see the youth-team pair oversee an improved performance, even if there was never any prospect of them being asked to do the job permanently.

I wasn't feeling too well the day after returning from West Brom, suffering from dizzy spells and a loss of appetite. Although it was probably no more than a 24-hour bug, I can't say the news filtering out of Loftus Road about the identity of the next incoming manager helped to make me feel much better. I'll be blunt here – whereas I'd been enthusiastic about Dowie's appointment, open-minded about Sousa and cautiously optimistic about Magilton, I thought Paul Hart was an absolute joke appointment from the beginning.

Hart had built his reputation as a youth coach, which would clearly be irrelevant to a board without the slightest interest in such things. However, he'd recently worked for some fairly unsavoury characters at Portsmouth and that, presumably, was the extent of his appeal – he was perceived as a yes man by Briatore's regime. What QPR clearly needed was someone to lift spirits after the circumstances of Magilton's exit – yet they plumped for one of the least inspirational characters in the game! The club hastily arranged a press conference at the last minute to announce Hart's appointment, which was attended by about four people. I wasn't among them because I had an appointment of my own – with the dentist. And, believe me, having my teeth scraped, picked at and subjected to a drill was probably less painful than half an hour in Hart's company would have been.

Those were my personal opinions of the new manager, but at the same time I thought it was important to maintain some balanced coverage of his appointment in the paper. Thumbing through Hart's CV, I saw that Tommy Williams – who had recently rejoined the club on loan – had played under him at Barnsley and done well, so I gave him a call. Williams was happy to talk up the new manager's qualities, not least because he was hoping to impress Hart all over again and earn himself a permanent deal at Loftus Road. Unfortunately for Williams, it turned out that he had just five games in which to catch Hart's eye!

I consider myself unfortunate as well, in that I attended all five of those games and the QPR performances were, at best, uninspiring. The manager didn't really do himself any favours with some of his post-match comments, stuff such as 'Rome wasn't built in a day' and his observation that there had been 'a lot of positives' after what turned out to be the only win of his tenure against Bristol City. There was nothing positive about Hart's tactics, with six defenders on the field in the closing stages as Rangers clung on to a 2-1 lead they hadn't remotely deserved. It ranked as the worst winning performance I'd ever seen by a QPR team since a shocking game at Reading some years earlier, when Mike Sheron's mis-struck shot bobbled off a defender's leg and into the net after the home side had dominated the game entirely. Hart just didn't appear to have any awareness of what he'd stumbled into. Not only were his team playing at home – they were a team that had been third in the league not too long ago! But the manager seemed to think he'd been brought in to try and avoid relegation – and, to give Hart credit, he did actually achieve that particular target after joining Crystal Palace later in the season.

There were plenty of boos from the crowd at that Boxing Day match, confirming to me that the fans' patience was fraying and, perhaps, having kept quiet on the subject of Briatore over the last few months, I should consider renewing the attack. A timely opportunity fell neatly into my lap a few days later when I picked up my copy of the match programme at Ipswich. Damien Delaney, who had moved to Portman Road the previous summer, was featured in the programme and gave some forthright opinions about the way his former club was being mismanaged by Briatore.

'If you run a football club like that, you've got no chance,' Delaney wrote. 'There's been no stability there since Flavio Briatore took over. You can't keep chopping and changing every five minutes, you need continuity, on and off the pitch.

'QPR have had seven managers in the last two years – they can't all be wrong. Look at Iain Dowie – he got sacked after 15 games. We were three points off second place. Crazy.

'The lads loved Dowie and if he was left in charge we would have got promoted to the Premier League. I guarantee you that.'

Not only was it refreshing to read Delaney's accurate appraisal of the Briatore regime – it looked far better to report the views of a player who had been at QPR at the time, rather than my own. Delaney's first-hand experience carried more weight for a start, and I didn't see how anyone at the club could reasonably grumble about us running a story around his comments when those were already in the public domain, so to speak.

Rangers played badly again, losing 3-0 and, while I waited around near the tunnel after the game, a supporter who'd been in one of the hospitality boxes – and, judging by his manner, had made the most of the hospitality, so to speak – emerged to have a slanging match with Ben Watson. It wasn't anything significant in itself, just another example of the frustration building up among QPR fans as they began to see through all the false promises. While the man from *The Sun* literally chased after Buzsaky in search of a juicy line, I managed to have a word with Adel Taarabt. I'm not really sure why, but some people seemed to think I wasn't a fan of Taarabt and I must say that really wasn't the case. He was friendly, good to talk to and, on his day, a magnificent player to watch. It concerned me that certain people at QPR had a tendency to over-indulge him and I didn't like the way some of my media colleagues built up the idea that he was the sole reason for the team's success the following season. In my view there were several other players who were just as key to that title success, but didn't always get the recognition they deserved. I certainly never found Taarabt arrogant or anything like that – on this occasion, in fact, he apologised for missing a couple of chances against Ipswich and pledged to put it right in the next game. That proved too tall an order – for the simple reason that Taarabt was left out for a predictably turgid FA Cup third-round tie at Sheffield United. With the match ending 1-1 and heavy snow scuppering QPR's next league game ahead of the replay, it meant the Blades provided the opposition for 60 per cent of Hart's matches in charge! The last of those was easily the liveliest of the three, with Rangers going three down and Taarabt coming off the bench to spark a late fightback before Sheffield United held on to win 3-2. Rumour had it that the Moroccan playmaker's dissatisfaction at his lack of game time under Hart contributed to the manager's resignation two days later, and whether that was true or not I honestly didn't care. In my book, Paul Hart's brief reign was just one more chapter in the tragi-comic farce QPR had become under Briatore.

This will probably sound like heresy of the highest degree, but I realised I was also becoming more and more indifferent to the team's results. It's something you can't possibly envisage when you become a football fan, the idea that you might not be too bothered whether your team wins or loses. Yet somehow all the nonsense that surrounded QPR and having to deal with it in my professional life as well had ground me down. Apart from that, I was looking at the long-term picture – ignoring one of footballers' favourite clichés, to take each game as it comes! The fans' frustration was clearly edging towards a tipping point and, as I saw it, if a couple more bad results brought them into open rebellion against the board, that had to be worth it in the long run. So to be honest, I wasn't exactly distraught when Dexter Blackstock – who would, but for Briatore's interference, have been leading the Rangers attack – scored one of the Nottingham Forest goals as they thrashed his former team 5-0. And, by the way, that in no way meant I didn't have a lot of sympathy for Mick Harford, who was back in charge of the team after Hart's departure. I liked Mick and thought he'd got a raw deal first time around, but he had little chance of arresting the slide this time – you could see the players' morale was rock bottom. As always, of course, the club's solution was to sign more and more of them, with Gianni going into overdrive to stockpile as many players as possible on short-term deals. Quashie had rejoined Rangers by then, while Wolves pair Carl Ikeme and Matt Hill arrived on loan. As for strikers, the club continued to scrape the bottom of the barrel ever more intensely, bringing in Marcus Bent – who didn't look fit – and then Tamas Priskin – who didn't look very good.

While I wasn't impressed by Gianni's recruits, I was even less impressed to read a feature that appeared in the *Daily Mirror* at around the same time. It's a generally accepted rule that unless, perhaps, a fellow journalist has written something offensive or unprofessional, you don't make public criticism of their work. With hindsight, I must admit I broke that rule by reacting to that *Mirror* interview with Briatore and describing it in less than glowing terms. My feeling at the time was – and still is – one of disappointment that a well-respected writer decided to accept Briatore's patently ludicrous explanations for the way he was running QPR. The tone of the piece suggested that Rangers fans should be eternally grateful to Briatore for buying the club and had no right to criticise 'because they pay £20'. Actually, of course, most of them were being charged a lot more and treated with utter contempt. As to the high turnover of QPR managers, Briatore astonishingly claimed that only one of them – Dowie – had been sacked!

I wrote an opinion piece in response to the feature, stressing again the damage Briatore had done to the club and why it would be best for him to leave. Having been posted online and then been picked up by fans' forums, my comments clearly came to the attention of the *Mirror* writer in question as well! When I next returned to the office after the weekend, I found a message to say that he'd called to speak to me – and presumably the reason hadn't been to offer his approval for my analysis of the situation. While he clearly knew Briatore far better than I did, I'm afraid it was evident he understood fairly little about QPR.

The Loftus Road crowd finally turned squarely against Briatore a few days after the Forest debacle, having witnessed another defeat, this time to struggling Scunthorpe. Hundreds of fans gathered outside the main entrance to demonstrate against Briatore and, in a sense, I was relieved to see that because it vindicated my own feelings towards the regime, as well as my response to the *Mirror* story. From talking to supporters' group representatives over the next few days, it was clear Briatore's throwaway '£20' remark had riled them as much as anything else. It underlined how drastically the lines of communication between board and supporters had been cut off – previously, for instance, the club had held fans' forums on a regular basis. Paul Finney, from the Independent Rs website, came up with a classic line when I spoke to him: 'They say they've got a four-year plan, yet they don't even seem to have a four-week plan.'

The only downside about the timing of the fans' demonstration was that it overshadowed Gareth Ainsworth's Loftus Road farewell. Gareth had returned to make an appearance on the pitch and wave goodbye – putting right something that I know the media department found greatly frustrating, with popular, long-serving players frequently departing via the back door. Quite rightly, he was afforded a great reception from the crowd and I devoted the best part of a page to an appreciation of his efforts the following week, running some quotes from Gareth alongside my own thoughts:

*On a day when QPR fans unleashed their deep discontent at the present state of the club, Ainsworth's farewell could only have served to remind them of better times.*

*For the veteran winger represented one of the last remaining links with an era when everyone connected with Rangers – manager, players, directors and supporters – genuinely pulled together and made each other proud.*

*Never mind that Ainsworth wasn't a Londoner, a homegrown product of QPR or a Rangers supporter. It seemed the club meant just as much to him as it did to every fan.*

*You knew he would cover every blade of grass, expend every ounce of sweat and do everything he could to inspire and encourage the players around him to strive for a result.*

*Off the field as well, Ainsworth was the club's cheerleader in chief, one of the players who would always stop to chat to fans, whether it was after a game or a gig with his band.*

*I don't think there can be a single Rangers fan who wouldn't thank Ainsworth for his service to our club and wish him all the very best at Wycombe.*

QPR's performances continued to slide over the next few weeks, and all of a sudden it was looking as though Paul Hart's assessment might not have been too wide of the mark. The team just couldn't pick up a point, even losing to bottom side Peterborough – after which I caught up again with Tommy Williams, now back at London Road after QPR had declined to make his move permanent. Williams revealed that the club had informed him they weren't prepared to sign any players, other than loans and short-term contracts until the summer, which didn't explain why they felt the need to sign quite so many of the above! Hearing that information also raised my hopes that perhaps Briatore might, after all, be preparing to pack his bags.

It wasn't quite as straightforward as that, but I think the increasing wave of hostility among the fans must have got through to Briatore in some respect – despite his considerable ego, it suddenly dawned on him that he had to be seen to take a back seat at the club. Belatedly, Briatore displayed some degree of PR awareness by announcing his resignation as chairman, with the Mittal family taking on a greater shareholding and Amit, in particular, taking a more prominent role. It was a masterstroke, to give Briatore his due!

The home game against Doncaster, 24 hours after Briatore's announcement, really felt like something of a watershed moment. The atmosphere around the stadium was noticeably improved, the fans chanted, 'We've got our Rangers back' and the team seemed to perform without the weight of the world on their shoulders at last. To crown the general feeling of euphoria, teenager Antonio German – already a familiar name on our sports pages through banging in the goals for Brent Schools – opening the scoring on his full debut for the club. It was wonderful to see that because Antonio represented everything that Briatore's regime had neglected in the shape of youth development, a community role model – and players being selected on merit. I remember beaming and punching the air with delight from the press box when Antonio hit the net. Brian Melzack, who was sitting nearby, said, 'I could see the difference in you today – it was like you were back!'

Brian was spot on – that was exactly how I felt. Rangers went on to win the game 2-1, their first victory since that abysmal Bristol City performance two months earlier, and I genuinely enjoyed watching them play again. Without Briatore's toxic influence taking centre stage, maybe there was renewed hope for the future of the club.

# 12

# HILL START CAN GET RANGERS MOVING

## (April 2010)

Two of Neil Warnock's favourite phrases, when in conversation, are, 'If I'm honest' and 'Are you with me?' So, if I'm honest, I must say I didn't find him an easy man to deal with when he was managing QPR. There's no doubt in my mind that Warnock's credentials at Championship level (and below) are pretty much unrivalled – the number of times he has built successful teams is staggering. To take over a club in such a sorry state – as Rangers were when he arrived in March 2010 – and turn them into league champions a year later was a remarkable feat. Purely as a QPR fan, you'd have to regard Warnock as a hero in that sense.

From my journalist's perspective, though, he could be hard work. Although he did tend to answer his phone more often than, say, John Gregory, there would often be an awful lot of fobbing off. 'Sorry pal, I'll have to let you go,' was another phrase I got used to hearing. And then there was his habit of going off at a tangent, trying to turn the conversation around to his own agenda – usually whichever football authority, fellow manager or chairman he was keen to either praise or condemn at the time. But the biggest obstacle to overcome during Warnock's tenure was that he would, at times, inexplicably place a total block on his players giving interviews. It was impossible to fathom when this might happen or why – Warnock's reasoning seemed to vary from wanting to prevent a negative line after a defeat, to making sure players kept their feet on the ground after a win, to some kind of superstition. Perhaps the most accurate reason, I suspect, was that he preferred to make things all about himself. Anyway, it was extremely frustrating and certainly made my job harder than it needed to be – even though, as Paul Morrissey informed me around the time of Warnock's arrival at QPR, the club had decided to lift the 'sanction' they'd imposed on me.

So that, in a nutshell, was my overall assessment of Neil Warnock. Are you with me?

A few days prior to Warnock's appointment, I'd had an interesting conversation with former Rangers right-back David Bardsley, who was seeking to advertise his own interest in the manager's job. Bardsley, who was coaching in Florida at the time, had been in touch with Tony Incenzo about throwing his hat in the ring and Tony asked if I'd be willing to help him do so. I didn't hesitate – not only was Bardsley a player I'd admired during his QPR career, I also thought it'd be seriously worth considering someone who already knew the club and understood what the supporters wanted. Yes, he hadn't actually been a manager before, but past experience isn't always as important as familiarity with the club and having a rapport with the fans – after all, Barcelona took a chance on Pep Guardiola and that didn't work out too badly! I rang Bardsley late one afternoon and we had a good chat – he made it clear he was deadly serious about his candidacy and convinced me, at any rate, that he'd have been capable of lifting QPR out of their alarming decline.

'You've got to have a nucleus of players who know what playing for that club is all about – that's what has been missing for years,' he told me. 'It kills me to see it, but I believe it's still possible to get back to those days.'

What Bardsley said was a theme I'd hear repeated over and over again by other members of the QPR side he enhanced. It meant something to those players, either because they were graduates of the youth team or because Rangers was the biggest club they'd played for at that time and that gave them extra incentive to prove themselves. In Bardsley's case, for instance, QPR were the club that turned him into an England international – and I would still argue he was at least as good as any other English right-back around at that time. However, while I enjoyed the chat with Bardsley and writing up the story, it was all too late to make any difference to his chances – Rangers' negotiations with Crystal Palace about a deal for Warnock were already too far down the line.

Anyway, I was impressed by Warnock the first time I met him, at the introductory press conference after his move from Palace was finalised. It helped that he was accompanied at Harlington by Mel Stein, a family friend who had been representing him. Mel introduced me to Warnock, as well to the new Rangers chairman Ishan Saksena, and both said all the right things. The manager came out with plenty of fighting talk, urging the more creative players in the QPR squad to mix it more and show leadership to stop the team hurtling towards the relegation zone. Saksena, meanwhile, responded to my query about reopening dialogue with Rangers supporters' groups very positively and I went away from the training ground with a lot more optimism than I'd felt in a long while.

It looked as though the new manager's enthusiasm had quickly rubbed off on the players as well, with back-to-back wins against West Brom and Plymouth lifting Rangers up the table. I rang Kevin Gallen to get his take on Warnock's appointment and, while impressed by the new man in his own right, he felt the key issue was that QPR finally had a manager in sole charge of team affairs. Warnock's predecessors, as he pointed out, had been undermined at every turn.

'I wouldn't have gone behind Gerry Francis's back, firstly because I had too much respect for him and also because I'd have been out the door!' he observed. 'It was Gerry who ran the team, nobody else. They've made it clear it's all down to Neil now, he'll have the full respect of the players. That's the way good football clubs are run.'

I couldn't have agreed more with Kev's analysis – and it wasn't just a matter of Briatore no longer sticking his nose in where it wasn't wanted. There was also another issue that had been damaging the club for so long, namely Gianni's conveyor belt of incoming players who had no shelf life and rarely resembled the manager's actual requirements. It would certainly be interesting to see whether a hard-nosed, experienced manager like Warnock tolerated that. And it was too early to say at the end of that season because, thanks to Gianni, QPR had already accumulated almost their full complement of loan signings permitted by the Football League! One or two of them had done well – Carl Ikeme, for example, put in some good displays in goal and made it clear he'd be keen to stay on, but Warnock already had another keeper in mind for next season.

One player who had moved on, unsurprisingly, was Raheem Sterling. The club took plenty of criticism for failing to hold on to a top prospect, but once Liverpool came calling there really wasn't a lot they could do other than cash in. Steve Gallen told me he'd never seen a player of Raheem's age offered the kind of contract Gianni had put on the table in an effort to keep him at QPR. Who knows, if the club had given greater priority to upgrading their youth set-up once the means were there to do so, it might have been a different matter.

The loss of Raheem certainly didn't reflect badly on Steve or his staff. I was also interested to learn that the only other club to make a formal offer for Raheem had been Fulham – but he'd turned them down flat!

After that initial Warnock bounce, the team's form dipped again and they went winless in seven games, albeit including a number of draws in that run. One of those brought a former QPR manager/coach back to Loftus Road – there were plenty of those knocking around in the Championship – in the shape of Paulo Sousa, now in charge of Swansea. One of Sousa's players, Nathan Dyer, found himself singled out for particular attention by the home crowd, keen to remind him of his conviction following an incident in which mobile phones had been stolen from a nightclub. Dyer, who had been sentenced to community service, nevertheless found himself subjected to chants of 'Nathan Dyer, you should be in jail' when the ball came his way. Unkind, yes, but one way of livening up a pretty dull affair – and, unfortunately, it was quite catchy too. So catchy, in fact, so that one member of the media continued singing it over and over again while he tapped away on his laptop in the press room after the game. Yet he'd made the cardinal error of sitting with his back to the door – and was so engrossed in his work that he remained blissfully unaware of Sousa's arrival for the post-match press conference. Cue one of those excruciating moments as the rest of the room fell silent, with Sousa treated to a solo musical rendition explaining exactly why one of his midfield players should have been unavailable for selection!

It all helped to lift the mood, anyway, which was also what I was aiming for when I decided to include an April Fool story in the sports section for the first time. As publication day fell on 1 April that year, it seemed worth taking the opportunity, so I concocted some nonsense about how QPR had enlisted the help of a Far East sports think-tank to redesign their kit for next season. Their study into the 'negative energy' channelled by particular colours, it was reported, had led them to advise Rangers to switch to an all-blue kit modelled on Chelsea's. Of course, the story wouldn't be complete without a comment, so I invented a 'spokesman' from QPR who observed, 'Having tried to sign virtually every player in the league and got no closer to our ambition of winning promotion, we need to try something different.'

I didn't get much response, to be honest – and, with hindsight, I suppose the fake story was a bit too credible, given some of the nonsense that the club had genuinely got entangled in during recent years. At that point, they also remained caught up in something else nobody wanted – a fight against relegation, and those concerns were deepened by a 4-0 thrashing at Leicester on Easter Monday. It set the stage nicely for Warnock's return to Selhurst Park and a vital clash against Crystal Palace, whose descent into administration had prompted him to make the move across London. There'd been little love lost between Warnock and Brendan Guilfoyle, the administrator at Palace, so I didn't imagine the QPR manager would be lost for words when I rang him ahead of the game. He'd always made it clear he enjoyed the verbal clashes and getting under people's skin as much as he could. I remember Ollie, who used to refer to Warnock as 'Mrs Doubtfire' during his time at Sheffield United, could get extremely wound up by his antics whenever the pair found themselves in adjacent dugouts. Warnock certainly didn't disappoint, hitting out at Guilfoyle while praising Palace and their fans at the same time and concluding, 'I'm sure I'll get some stick, but that's normal most places I go! If you ask the Palace supporters who they'd trust, Neil Warnock or the administrator, I don't think there'd be too many on the other side.'

It wasn't too surprising that Warnock seemed to motivate his players more effectively than Paul Hart, who was shrouded in gloom just for a change as Rangers overcame his side 2-0, helped by a towering performance from Peter Ramage in central defence. Ramage was one of the nicest blokes in the squad and, although he hadn't had too much praise come his way up to then, really rose to the occasion after Damion Stewart had gone off injured in the first minute. I spoke to Ramage afterwards and he was still beaming about the victory, which he dedicated to the stricken Stewart.

The Selhurst Park win gave Rangers enough momentum to scramble over the line in terms of avoiding relegation and, from speaking to Warnock, he was evidently impatient to begin building his own team straight away. The top items on the manager's shopping list weren't all that startling a revelation, either – 'I'd like to spend most of my summer trying to get forwards in, we've got a little bit missing up front. We've not had a target man since I've been here – they've all been out on loan!'

Interestingly, Warnock seemed unconvinced as to the wisdom of a permanent deal for the player he always referred to as 'Tarra-bat'. At times he'd indicated an intention to build around the Moroccan the following season, but then swiftly played down the possibility, saying there'd be other options. However, one new face he was determined to secure was Palace defender Clint Hill – something David McIntyre alerted me to even before the season was over. We ran David's story on the back page – and then had to do it again after a major systems failure at Archant on the Tuesday afternoon. Without greater technical knowledge, I can't really describe it other than to say the paper's templates, page furniture and so on just disappeared into a black hole! The IT help desk predicted it could take them up to 24 hours to repair the damage, so we had to put together a makeshift two pages on a different server ahead of the print deadline. I won't pretend the final product was all that impressive, but we did at least get the story of Rangers' move for Hill in – and what a move that turned out to be in the long run.

There were a few more bits and pieces to wrap up before the end of what had been a trying season, one way or another. We ran a full page feature on Rangers' Under-18s' League Cup final success – partly to showcase the good work Steve Gallen and his team had been doing and partly because I was encouraged to see the new chairman, alongside Warnock, among the spectators. That also suggested, I hoped, that youth development was something QPR might finally take seriously again. A couple of weeks later, I managed to complete a Gallen hat-trick by attending the League One play-off final at Wembley, with Millwall – where Joe was now assistant to Kenny Jackett – defeated Swindon to return to the Championship. It was great to see the pair of them enjoying some success and Joe admitted that he'd started thinking about next season's meetings with QPR as soon as the final whistle blew!

To be truthful, I wasn't really looking ahead to next season with anything like the eagerness Joe Gallen was. Although things had improved at the club in recent months, I still felt a kind of mental fatigue and, again, some of the other sporting distractions of the summer break looked more attractive than trying to keep up with events at QPR. There was the prospect of watching Adam Gilchrist star for Middlesex under the Lord's floodlights, James DeGale's career was now moving towards professional titles and an eventual collision course with his fiercest rival, George Groves. And there was another World Cup tournament just around the corner, although I can't really remember anything about whatever supplement we had to put together. I'm sure they thought better of plastering John Terry all over the front cover this time, though!

Without going into too much detail, it's also fair to say that much of my energy and focus at around this time was taken up by family issues. These included the sadness of bereavement and the high of a wedding, but also the roots of a deeply painful, wide-reaching falling-out in my family. My closest friends – and most relatives – will know exactly what I'm talking about and are also aware that this deep-seated rift can never be healed because one individual will never allow it to be. As I said, this isn't the place for in-depth psychoanalysis, but I didn't deal with any of this until a few years later, when I sought counselling and I now realise how the whole affair affected my state of mind at the time. I feel it certainly made me an angrier person – someone who was quicker to blow up at minor setbacks, quicker to get frustrated and quicker to give up on things, maybe on people as well. I think there were ways in which that influenced my decision to make the following season my final one as the paper's QPR correspondent.

However, I did realise there were many other Rangers fans who were impatiently awaiting the arrival of the 2010-11 season – or, sooner than that, the publication of the fixture list. In recent years, the release of the fixtures has somehow morphed into a major sports news event, with every media outlet frantically seeking various ways to cover it but also trying to avoid forking out the fee due to Football DataCo for publishing the actual list. This fervour can result in some utterly banal journalism and a waste of everyone's time. I've yet to meet any football fan who genuinely wants to read anything about fixtures beyond the fixture list itself. Incredibly, during my final year with Archant, the sports staff all received a directive from the company's self-styled online guru that he wanted a piece published on each club, entitled 'Seven things we learned from the fixture list'. It ranks as one of the most idiotic ideas I've ever encountered – even now, I'm struggling to comprehend how he could have meant this seriously. Seven? Correct me if I'm wrong, but you learn precisely one thing from fixture publication – which matches are scheduled for which dates in the calendar. End of conversation! Thanks for that genius idea, Captain Clickbait.

With all that said, I couldn't ignore 'Fixtures Release Day' entirely. So I decided to go for a tongue-in-cheek look at what QPR fans could expect on the day the fixtures were due out – making broad predictions about Rangers' likely schedule based on what we'd seen in recent seasons. My forecasts were:

An opening-day home game against unfashionable opposition – tick! Barnsley again, as it turned out.

An unattractive home game against one of the Championship's worst-supported teams over the Christmas and New Year period – cross! Swansea and Bristol City didn't really fall into that category.

One of the last two games would be against another promotion candidate, but ultimately meaningless – cross! Leeds did fit that description, but there'd be plenty still hanging in the balance on that final day.

At least one lengthy away trip in midweek, probably to Burnley or one of the Welsh clubs – tick! Swansea was a Tuesday night in October, although the Turf Moor date turned out to be a weekend.

A blank weekend at the end of January (FA Cup fourth-round weekend) – tick! An absolute banker for QPR, although they did rearrange a league game to fill the date instead.

The whole thing was intended as a bit of light-hearted silliness, which I don't think does any harm now and then. It's easy to get bogged down when you're constantly writing stuff with a more serious tone – and there hadn't been too much of a QPR flavour to laugh about in the last couple of years. Laugh at, perhaps.

Although, as I said, Warnock wasn't averse to fobbing me off over the phone, he was quite good that summer and I was able to keep reasonably well updated on the club's progress in the transfer market. Darren Ambrose was the player we spoke about most during the close season – he'd scored the goal that kept Palace up at Sheffield Wednesday's expense and Warnock was desperate to bring him to Loftus Road. 'I think I will get Ambrose at one stage or another because he's in the last year of his contract,' the manager said, while repeating his mantra of wanting to sign more forwards. That didn't bode well for some of the strikers who were out of favour at Loftus Road, although I spoke to Patrick Agyemang just before pre-season and he reiterated his desire to fight for a place in Warnock's team. In a sense, although the club had already signed Jamie Mackie and Leon Clarke, Agyemang was right not to be despondent about his prospects – the way Warnock operated, there was every chance of four or five forwards being involved on matchday. Rowan Vine, on the other hand, was quite open in admitting his QPR career was over – Warnock had informed him he wasn't part of his plans and the club were negotiating to cancel the final year of his contract. Personally, I was sorry to see Vine go – he'd been really flying until he broke his leg and just hadn't been given much opportunity to fight his way back into the side after returning. In a way, that was hardly surprising at a club where a year was comfortably long enough for the entire coaching and playing personnel to be revamped, maybe even twice.

For reasons I've outlined, I wasn't able to get to many of Rangers' pre-season matches, but there wasn't any excuse not to watch them in action at Boreham Wood, the nearest ground to where I live! It was a useful exercise for me – literally as I could walk to Meadow Park – but also because it gave me the chance to meet Warnock's number two, Mick Jones. Mick had worked with Warnock for years at various clubs and was fairly old-school – which meant that, in football terms, he knew his stuff and he didn't mind talking to the local paper. I felt it'd be useful to build an alternative contact on the coaching side – something I'd not really had at QPR since the days when Gary Waddock and Alan McDonald were the men in charge. I spoke to Mick at length about several matters – Lee Cook's recent injury, the latest on the move for Ambrose and the question that had rumbled on for several months, would Taarabt be returning? Mick suggested that the pendulum might now be swinging back towards yes, with Taarabt looking unlikely to secure a dream move to one of the giants of La Liga.

'My advice would be that, if he wants to get to the top, then he should sign for QPR,' said Mick. 'Neil Warnock will help him get to the top. The way Neil would manage him, he'd be perfect for him. All I can say is that Neil's still trying to sign him and I think he should sign – it'd be a good move for his career.'

Before the season began, there was still time for me to get back to Wembley Arena and see if QPR could defend their London Masters title. I was intrigued to see how many of the team from 2009 would be back in hoops again – and, although Andy Sinton had defected to Spurs this time, there were plenty of familiar faces. It felt as if some of them, like Marcus Bignot and Simon Royce, had been QPR players a bit too recently to qualify for a Masters shirt! But the ex-Rangers rose to the occasion once more, recovering a 3-0 deficit against West Ham to draw the final and then triumph on penalties. I was able to get a word with Michael Meaker, who had scored a hat-trick in the final – perhaps not surprising, as he was still turning out in the Southern League at the time – and also spoke to Wayne Fereday, a player I remembered from my early visits to Loftus Road.

I used those interviews in the sports section rather than holding onto them for any kind of new season supplement – because we didn't do one. It just wasn't a subject that ever came up for discussion and, frankly, there weren't many opportunities for gathering the relevant material. I suppose my reasoning was that, if Warnock managed to turn QPR into promotion winners overnight, we could always produce a supplement at the end of the season instead!

# 13

# BACK IN THE BIG TIME

## (May 2011)

It would be hard to argue that the 2010-11 season shouldn't be regarded among the most successful in QPR's history. The team won more than half of their league fixtures, losing only six, and spent the entire season in the top two, marching back to the Premier League for the first time in 15 years. It was a remarkable transformation for a club that had talked the talk, but spectacularly failed to walk the walk during the previous three seasons. So why exactly did it all leave me – a lifelong Rangers fan – feeling cold?

Thinking about it, the answer is hard to pinpoint. One factor, I think, is that I didn't feel any emotional connection to the team that won the Championship. It was overwhelmingly a newly-assembled team, containing several good professionals but none – with the exception of Danny Shittu, who returned to play a fringe role in the second half of the season – who had any particular affection for the club. It was a complete contrast to what I'd witnessed in the 2004 promotion season when, leaving aside professional pride, it had been evident how much it mattered to the players and management.

Then there was the issue of how frustrating it became trying to write about the team when your access to players appeared to be completely at Neil Warnock's whim. There was no apparent rhyme or reason – and, yes, I had enough of their phone numbers in my book to get by. But, from the journalist's perspective, the whole point of travelling to matches is the opportunity to pick up a post-match interview or two. However entertaining the football might have been, drawing a blank in terms of match reaction feels like a wasted afternoon or evening.

However, the worst thing about that season was the way promotion was tarnished by the Alejandro Faurlin affair. It ended up being probably the grubbiest Championship success in history – and was directly a result of the way the club had been run for years. After hopes had been raised by Briatore's decision to stand down as chairman the previous season, this was a nasty reminder that he hadn't gone away and would doubtless now bask in the glory of promotion. There was no celebratory parade at the end of the season, which underlined how the owners viewed this as a triumph for themselves rather than for QPR supporters. I was acutely aware, though, that further attacks on the board would fall on generally deaf ears now that the team were finally successful on the pitch. It had been a different matter when Rangers were floundering in the Championship. That's the inescapable truth about the vast majority of football fans – and I'm not criticising this – but, to put it simply, they want to see their team winning and everything else is secondary. So I suppose, as the end of the season approached, I was struck by a growing realisation that it was time for me to take a step back from QPR.

The issue of speaking to players post-match raised its head as soon as the season had begun with a 4-0 victory against Barnsley at Loftus Road. Although the margin of the win had been flattering, Warnock's new-look team had produced some good football and the signs were encouraging. I really couldn't fathom why, according to Messrs Taylor and Morrissey, he'd put a block on media requests for players. Whatever the reason, I quickly slipped out of the ground and approached Jamie Mackie – who had just scored on his debut – on his way to the car park. I don't really like badgering people in the street – if I did, maybe becoming a political journalist would have been a more sensible career choice – but it was either that or going back from a resounding home win without any player reaction. Being the kind of bloke he is, Mackie didn't mind at all, which made me wonder why Warnock would have issued instructions to the media department, but not to the team. There was nothing controversial to be written – in fact, Mackie's message was along the lines of 'don't get carried away after one match', which was, as far as I could gather, what the manager wanted to come across.

I don't think anyone was in danger of getting carried away at that point. In fact, the match that convinced me Rangers were destined for an extraordinary season was, ironically, the only one among the first eight that they failed to win. It's funny how frequently games against Derby seem to be pivotal to QPR's fortunes – and the visit to Pride Park at the end of August was a case in point.

Recovering a 2-0 deficit in injury time, with Patrick Agyemang getting the first before Mackie struck the equaliser to reveal both the team's fighting spirit and his own impressive display of what many tattooed folk describe as body art, was highly significant. I spoke to Kaspars Gorkss afterwards – although obviously I had to intercept him en route to the team bus – and he described the comeback as a 'miracle'. That might seem something of an exaggeration, but at the same time it was hard to envisage a QPR side in recent years that would have pulled off that kind of comeback.

Aside from that 2-2 draw, Warnock's team just kept on winning – and, at the same time, the stance on player interviews continued more often than not. As a result, it also became clear that someone in the press room at Loftus Road was out to make trouble for me. I believe I know who it was – not a club employee, I should stress – but I'm none the wiser as to their motivation. After another home victory and the usual enquiry about player interviews, the message came back from Matt Webb – at that time the most junior member of the media department – that there wouldn't be any. I think I said something like, 'This is just getting ridiculous, Matt,' in response, and I said it with plenty of frustration, but without shouting and certainly not attacking him personally in any way. Apart from anything else, Matt is one of the nicest blokes I've ever met. He's a QPR supporter and I'd first met him more than a year earlier, when he was seeking work experience after completing his university course. I can't remember how many weeks he spent with us, but it was great to have him around and clear then that he had an aptitude for media work. I was delighted when I heard he'd been given a role at QPR and he went on to become editor of the club's award-winning matchday programme.

Anyway, I was somewhat shocked to get a call from Paul Morrissey the following Monday, asking about an 'incident' in the press room – to my astonishment it had been reported to him that I'd had a real go at Matt and yelled at him. Paul asked if I'd ring Matt to smooth over anything that might need smoothing over, which I was more than happy to do – and he seemed just as bemused as I was as to where this had come from. While I was thoroughly relieved to hear Matt confirm there was no problem between us, it wasn't particularly nice to realise someone had been busy stirring.

I did lose my temper with Paul over the same issue later in the season, however. At that time, Brian Melzack had been running a pre-match broadcast for QPR

World – the idea was to build up to the live commentary, provided by BBC London, with some discussion and chat about the club. I was happy to help Brian out, so when he was unwell at the last minute and couldn't get to the Bristol City home game on the New Year Bank Holiday the SOS to fill in came my way. That meant getting along to the ground a fair bit earlier than planned, but no problem – I did the broadcast with Brian's co-presenter and it seemed to go well. The match itself appeared to be going well too – with Rangers 2-1 up until Steven Caulker, later to don the hooped shirt, levelled in the final minute. That, it turned out, was the putative trigger for post-match interviews to be refused and I wasn't slow to let Paul know my feelings on the subject. I thought it more than a bit rich that after I'd put myself out to do a favour for the club they weren't prepared to help me. 'I'll try and sort out something over the phone tomorrow,' Paul promised – but Bank Holidays often played havoc with the schedule and I knew I'd be really pressed for time the next day, so that wasn't ideal. Warnock might be fast earning his place in the pantheon of all-time QPR heroes, but he was also being an utter pain in the backside.

By and large, I was able to accumulate enough interviews over the phone to get by, but the uncertainty over matchdays meant I ended up skipping the majority of Rangers' away games unless they were relatively close to home. Nottingham Forest, Hull and Blackburn in the FA Cup were the only mid-to-long-distance ones I attended that season. Forest was one I never wanted to miss, just in case it turned out to be QPR's first win at the City Ground! Which, of course, it never did until some years later. But the reality was that most of these trips were no longer cost-effective if you couldn't guarantee returning home with useful content – and the Archant attitude towards expenses had changed drastically since my early days with the company, in line with economic circumstances. Of course, there'd been a time when being out of pocket on a QPR away game wouldn't have bothered me too much – as a fan, I'd just wanted to see the team play, but that raw enthusiasm had filtered out of me over the last couple of years. Another factor to keep in mind was that, because of QPR's impressive start to the season, they'd shot up the pecking order in terms of live TV coverage. So again – and this was very much in line with my employers' thinking – why not just save money and cover the game off TV if you're getting the same material as you'd probably get from a 400-mile round trip?

The other important point to make about this situation is the effect of making it far harder to establish personal recognition with new players – and, at Rangers, being a 'new' player usually only lasted about six months on average. Over the years, most players – apart from the likes of Gareth Ainsworth, Marc Bircham and Lee Cook – probably wouldn't remember my name, but they did know my face. Because they'd remember doing interviews with me by the team coach or at the training ground. Once that wasn't happening, I became no more than a voice on the phone – and suddenly the situation is then more formal, an interview as opposed to a chat, a conversation. You might think that makes little difference, but it wasn't the way I'd always operated and it wasn't the way I preferred to operate, particularly with regard to QPR. For me, it was all about trying to build relationships and trust as best I could and that was now becoming more and more difficult.

Warnock had repeatedly made clear you could never have too many strikers in his opinion – so it was inevitable he'd add more to his squad before the transfer window closed at the end of August. Around that time, I spoke to Otis Roberts, the uncle of Jason Roberts and an influential figure in the foundation his nephew had set up to help underprivileged children – both in his native Grenada and in Brent, where he'd grown up. The foundation did fantastic work, which we did our best to help publicise – and I was also quite happy to help get it into the public domain that Jason, who was playing for Blackburn at the time, was interested in joining QPR. I thought he'd have been a brilliant signing for Rangers – not only in light of his strong record of winning promotion from the Championship, but also because he was a local boy who had done it the hard way, starting out in non-league football and working his way up. When Ollie was QPR manager, I'd definitely have rung him to see if he was interested – and, having already managed Jason at Bristol Rovers, I'm sure he would have been. I didn't think there'd be much point in trying that with Warnock.

In fairness to the manager, I couldn't complain about the quality of the forward players he did bring in ahead of the deadline – Rob Hulse and Tommy Smith. Personally, I rated Hulse as one of the best target men in the Championship, one of the players I had no doubt would be a success at QPR. How wrong can you be? Although he arrived with injury problems, it's still something of a mystery to me that the move never worked out. Smith, too, came with a good track record – a wily player with the knowhow to play anywhere in that area between midfield

*Wayne Routledge was an exciting addition to the QPR forward line, as well as turning out to be a better interviewee than I'd been led to believe.*

*You certainly couldn't have predicted the 'QPR Champions' message would be on display little more than a year after Neil Warnock's move across London from Crystal Palace. The 2010-11 season was a memorable one for Rangers fans... and yet I just felt more and more detached from it all as the title-winning campaign progressed.*

*Warnock has to be among the best managers of all time at Championship level – but I'm not sure it's advisable for someone of his vintage to go around in shorts all the time.*

*Relief as much as jubilation... the untidy saga of the Faurlin transfer meant Rangers had the threat of a points deduction hanging over them until the final day of that season.*

*On the field at least, QPR secured the Championship title with this 2-0 win at Watford in their penultimate game of the season. By then, I felt like, to coin a phrase, 'the only one at a party who's sober'.*

*With two loan spells before his permanent switch from Tottenham in 2010, Moroccan playmaker Adel Taarabt played under plenty of QPR managers! John Gorman, assistant manager to Jim Magilton, is looking on during this game against Plymouth.*

Picture: Dave Brennan

The flair of Taarabt (above, in action against Portsmouth) was one of the main factors behind Rangers' Championship success in 2010-11 and he celebrated (below) at Watford by wrapping himself in a national flag. While Warnock seized any opportunity to gush about the player, he never managed to pronounce his name correctly!

Picture: Dave Brennan

*Warnock usually surrounds himself with very capable coaching staff such as Keith Curle (L), the two of them watching avidly here from the Loftus Road touchline.*

*Arguably Warnock's most influential signings were those who followed him to QPR from Palace – Clint Hill and Shaun Derry (pictured), the latter forming a productive partnership in central midfield with Alejandro Faurlin.*

*Behind the mask... the strange feeling of reporting on a match at a virtually-deserted Loftus Road during the Covid-19 pandemic in 2020.*

*It fell to former Watford player Tommy Smith to score the goal that sealed Rangers' promotion to the Premier League at Vicarage Road.*

Picture: Dave Brennan

*Even if I wasn't feeling boundless enthusiasm for QPR's return to the top level, I enjoyed putting together the Times promotion supplement to mark the occasion!*

and attack. I even once asked the manager if Smith could be an option at centre-forward. 'Play him up top – are you joking? I'd put my missus there first, if I'm honest,' was Warnock's withering response.

Inevitably, the club managed to botch Smith's transfer from Portsmouth, failing to complete the paperwork in time to register him as a QPR player, which meant they had to sign him on loan instead. It was a timely reminder that, while Rangers' fortunes on the pitch had swiftly been transformed, the same people were still overseeing a shambles behind the scenes. The club hadn't changed anything like as much as was needed – and, right on cue, Briatore then re-emerged to prove that he certainly hadn't changed. During an interview with an Italian magazine, he declared his ambition – a favourite word, of course – to appoint Marcello Lippi as QPR manager if the team reached the Premier League. The timing was perfect, coinciding with Rangers extending their unbeaten start to the season and equalling a club record. As I've probably made clear, I wasn't a paid-up member of the Neil Warnock fan club, but he certainly deserved more respect than he'd been afforded by those comments about Lippi. I subsequently learned that, after the team had lost a couple of matches later in the season, Briatore rang the manager and threatened him with the sack. Unbelievable. I dusted down my back page comment template, but this time with a change in tone. I tried to stress how much better things had been since Briatore took a less prominent role but also pointed out – channelling Ollie to some extent – that, rather like a persistent weed in your garden, the odious ex-chairman hadn't gone away entirely. QPR could become successful, but not with Briatore running the show.

Some of Warnock's decisions that season turned out to be absolute masterstrokes. Handing the captain's armband to Taarabt after Fitz Hall's injury early in the season was certainly a gamble, you could argue, but it seemed to get the best out of him. Another that worked out well was the idea of deploying Mackie as an emergency right-back when injuries meant the options were limited. At the same time, there were other situations that made little sense – for example, Warnock's apparent blind spot when it came to Martin Rowlands. It seemed he would go to any lengths not to play Rowlands – pushing defenders into midfield instead for the game at Leeds just before Christmas, which finished in a 2-0 defeat. Thinking about it, I was just relieved to get home in one piece!

I'd travelled to Elland Road with my good friend Marc, a Leeds supporter – shrugging off the doom-laden forecasts of heavy snowfall later that day.

We drove to Stevenage and caught the train up to Leeds, where the weather was chilly but sunny – not a flake of snow in sight – and we wondered what all the fuss had been about. Returning south later, we began to realise the warnings might not have been so wide of the mark – the landscape was thickly covered in white and conditions on the road far from ideal. However, we set off cautiously along the motorway, with the seat warmers switched on for a bit of extra comfort. One of the scariest moments of my life then followed as we passed underneath a bridge, just as an enormous lorry dumped an even bigger deluge of snow all over the windscreen. Suddenly you couldn't see a thing! I've no idea how Marc managed to keep his head and control the car, but somehow we escaped unscathed. 'You know what?' I said. 'I don't need the seat heater on any more. That's warmed my arse up more than enough!'

I should have known Rangers were fated to lose. There's been history ever since I've known Marc and our mutual friend Justin, also a Leeds fan – who I accompanied to a 4-0 drubbing at Elland Road during our student days. Some years later, all three of us went to the game and I made the mistake of observing, 'It can't be as bad as last time.' Fate and the veteran striker Brian Deane must have overheard me, with the latter scoring four times in Leeds's 6-1 victory.

Anyway, like many other fans, I was sorry to see Rowlands' QPR career grinding to a halt. Rowly had been the last remaining link with Rangers' 2004 promotion side and, but for bad luck with injuries, he'd surely have got an opportunity to play in the Premier League. I'd have liked to ask him about it, but he wasn't ever the most enthusiastic of interviewees! I don't mean he had an attitude or anything like that, he just didn't feel particularly comfortable about talking to the media, which is fair enough – you can't expect every footballer to enjoy that aspect of the job.

I suppose another thing that disappointed me about Warnock was his apparent willingness to go along with whatever players Gianni foisted on him. Obviously his predecessors had all had to endure the same thing – some to a more absurd degree than others – but I'd hoped a strong-minded, opinionated character like Warnock might not stand for it. The manager was at least getting the players he did actually want – Clint Hill, Shaun Derry, Paddy Kenny and Rob Hulse were all evidence of that – but he didn't seem to have an issue with extra arrivals like Georgios Tofas. The Cypriot winger turned up on a free transfer in November, with the manager admitting, 'I know we don't desperately need someone in that position, but it's worth a shout.'

Tofas ended up playing half an hour of first-team football that season, so it probably hadn't been worth a shout. Inevitably there were further bizarre arrivals as soon as January rolled around, including Norwegian midfielder Petter Vaagan Moen and Pascal Chimbonda, who had been out of favour at Blackburn. Neither of them were called upon to play that much, but Warnock didn't appear to mind. Granted, at least the manager was no longer receiving instructions from the boardroom on which team to pick – but why were these players there in the first place?

With that said, I didn't mind making an exception in the case of Shittu, who Gianni brought back to the club at the end of January. I bumped into him at Hull, where he'd travelled with the team, although he wasn't match fit, and it was really nice to see big Dan again. He hadn't changed much – he still had that tendency to break into laughter quite easily, but I knew he was deadly serious about wanting to kick-start his career back at QPR. As he reminded me, he'd done his cruciate ligament midway through the 2004 promotion season – I remember watching that game, at Bournemouth – and felt as though he'd missed out in a way. I'm glad that in the end he did get to make up for lost time, featuring in the Rangers team that made certain of promotion six years later – against his old club Watford, as well.

The only blip for Dan arrived a few matches into his QPR comeback, getting himself sent off against another of his former clubs, Millwall, where he'd later go back to finish his career. Needless to say, he got some verbals from the crowd at the Den that night – as, it seems, does every player with the effrontery to leave Millwall and pull on another team's shirt! It was one of Rangers' rare defeats that season, a match in which anyone looking for Taarabt would have been advised to check the pockets of Millwall midfielder Jimmy Abdou. That, however, didn't deter one of my media colleagues from wasting Warnock's time afterwards with a series of questions inviting him to talk up Taarabt's star credentials. Warnock, who was always inclined to advance his own agenda rather than other people's, refused to bite – but the guy wasn't discouraged. He must have written his story already, because as soon as Kenny Jackett arrived in the press room, he was greeted with something along the lines of, 'You must be delighted to have beaten a team with the quality of Taarabt, Kenny?'

It's an easy cliché when people refer to 'lazy journalism', but this really was a good example of precisely that and I've no time for it. Someone's been assigned to cover a game, he does the minimum of research and decides in advance who the story will be about. All he needs are the quotes to back up his pre-conceived idea. Why bother going to the match at all if what you see on the pitch has no bearing on what you write? Why not ask Millwall's manager to comment on his own player's performance? But no, it's been decided that Taarabt's got to be the story, even though he's had one of his quietest games all season. I felt quite sorry for Taarabt with some of the ludicrous questions he had to answer in interviews that season – I remember overhearing an experienced national broadcaster ask him what superstitions he had. 'Adel, do you always put on your left boot before your right?'

I suppose sometimes you're just searching for a different angle and it doesn't always work out as you'd hoped. That was something I discovered myself midway through the season, when a cold snap meant QPR's game was called off at short notice. Wondering how I'd fill up space in the sports section, I realised Rangers' next fixture would be against Watford – whose home game against Leicester had survived the freezing weather. So if I could wangle myself into the press box at Vicarage Road, I might be able to come up with a story looking ahead to their clash with QPR.

Watford won 3-2, and in the end the angle was an obvious one – their long-serving full-back Lloyd Doyley had scored the only goal of his career against Rangers a year earlier, during the game that ultimately led to Jim Magilton's dismissal. So I explained my thinking to Watford's press officer and asked her if it might be possible to grab a word with their player after the game. She was quite happy to oblige and Doyley duly recounted his goal, stressed that he'd rather beat QPR again than score for a second time, and gave me some good quotes about his former team-mates, Tommy Smith and Heidar Helguson, into the bargain. All good – and I didn't think anything of it at the time when the press officer stood by Doyley, holding out a dictaphone while he was speaking. That was becoming fairly standard practice among club media staff and I could see why – they wanted to have a record of exactly what their player had said in case they were misquoted or spoke about a controversial subject. I didn't feel quite the same a couple of days later when I spotted a story on Watford's website about Doyley – yes, recalling his goal against QPR and looking ahead to their trip to Loftus Road! All quotes in response to the questions I'd asked him. I wouldn't have minded if she'd given me any inkling that Watford wanted to run the interview – I'm sure we could have arranged a day and time to suit everyone. As it was almost Christmas – and to tweak another cliché – I abandoned any plans I might have had to post a card bearing compliments of the season to Vicarage Road.

All of this did contribute to my general feeling of frustration, but it's also important to stress that certain aspects of the job continued to be enjoyable and fulfilling. Chris Ampofo, who had been a West Ham youth-team player, was particularly proactive in his role as chairman of the Brent Schools FA and, mainly thanks to him, we were able to give district football a fair bit of coverage in the paper. One name that kept cropping up in the weekly reports was that of Ricky German – Antonio's younger brother – who played for the under-12 team and broke a Brent record for the most consecutive hat-tricks. So it was nice to write something about the family as a whole, with quotes from the boy's mum, and highlighting the pathway that was there for promising young players in the area, something that Raheem Sterling had already shown. I was really pleased for Ricky and the rest of his team-mates that they got to walk out on the Loftus Road pitch after winning the county cup later in the season – the QPR Community Trust had got involved and arranged a presentation at half-time during Rangers' game against Crystal Palace. Peter Ramage, who had been out injured, presented the boys with the trophy. Peter always came across as a really genuine bloke, even the time when I tried to be slightly mischievous during a phone interview. It was around the time Briatore's name had become mud in the motorsport world – obviously, in my book, it had been mud for some time – and the QPR squad had all been informed they were not to comment on the matter under any circumstances.

I actually wanted to get up to speed on Peter's progress returning from injury, but I couldn't resist opening with, 'So anyway, Formula 1. What's your take on it all?'

There was silence on the other end of the line. I could almost visualise Peter's face frozen in horror, wondering what on earth he could say. And he was such a nice fellow, I had to give up on it and admit I'd been kidding. The relief was palpable in his voice!

Writing features on past QPR players was also something I'd been doing a lot more of – I suppose the opportunity to chat about the club's history was a way of blocking out the more recent stuff, in a sense. Tony Incenzo was enormously helpful with that – he was in contact with a lot of ex-Rangers and delved into his contacts book for me on numerous occasions. Ian Dawes was the first former player I profiled that season, looking back at the side he'd helped to win the old Division Two title in 1983 and discussing the importance of a settled back four. Through my perspective as a boy, Dawes was synonymous with the left-back position at QPR, in the same way right-back Warren Neill and goalkeeper Peter Hucker had been. With that said, I hadn't been aware of just how consistent Dawes was until I looked up his career stats – he'd featured in every single Rangers game for four and a half years during the mid-80s!

I ran a number of similar features over the next few months, speaking to Don Givens, Dave Thomas and Ian Gillard – all stars of the Rangers team that had come so close to the league championship in 1976. Gillard was particularly interesting to speak to – and what he told me was a fairly shocking indictment of the club's attitude towards ex-players at the time. He'd rung the club to ask about the possibility of coming to a game at Loftus Road and been given short shrift – effectively he was told to go and buy a ticket like everyone else! This to a guy who had given the club 14 years' outstanding service and represented them at international level as well. It's such a relief to see how their attitude has completely transformed in recent years, with Andy Sinton playing a big part in the Forever Rs club that invites former players back to Loftus Road on a regular basis.

One anniversary I certainly couldn't let pass came at the end of March – 25 years since one of my favourite childhood footballing memories. The Easter Monday when QPR walloped Chelsea 6-0 at Loftus Road! By then it was evident – at least, until the Faurlin investigation began to cast doubt over Rangers' elevation to the Premier League – that the club would again be facing Chelsea on equal terms the following season. So I spoke to Steve Wicks, who played in the centre of QPR's defence that day but also had two spells with Chelsea and was well-placed to analyse not only the game, but the relationship between the clubs.

'We were always perceived as the smaller club and that day felt like we'd taught big brother a lesson,' said Wicks. 'Some of the Chelsea players were full of themselves, they thought they were better than they were.

'But QPR always used to beat them. When we had our best side of that period under Terry Venables, they weren't even in our division.

'The 6-0 became almost a mental thing for Chelsea. When I was playing for them a year or two later at Loftus Road, there were still a lot of players who'd been involved in that game and they went onto the plastic pitch with trepidation.'

If space had been no object, I could probably have filled a couple of pages with Steve Wicks and his reminiscences of that glorious day when Chelsea were put to the sword!

Like most people, the first I knew of the Faurlin affair was when news broke, just before that Palace game in March, that the FA had charged QPR with seven misdemeanours relating to the Argentinian midfielder's transfer. My initial reaction? A sense of extreme exasperation and 'here we go again' just about covers it, I suppose. Innocent until proven guilty is, of course, a bedrock of the English system. With that said, I just couldn't see how the club could wriggle out of this one, knowing the slapdash way in which they'd tended to operate. It just infuriated me that, irrespective of the eventual outcome, the name of Queens Park Rangers was being dragged through the mud yet again. Guns in the boardroom. The Great Brawl of China. Briatore's posturing and interference in team affairs. Fleecing fans for £50 a head. The Magilton/Buzsaky incident at Watford. It seemed never-ending and this was the point where I began to feel I'd just had enough. I didn't want to be around the club. I found it impossible to enjoy the performances on the pitch, knowing the nonsense that had gone on off it for years. Not surprisingly, I was turning into a complete killjoy at matches and I'm sure that showed! David McIntyre – who has stoically born the killjoy tag for far longer than me! – summed it up perfectly at one game when he said to me, 'It's like being the only one at a party who's sober.'

I decided to raise the subject with my colleagues on the sports desk – who, it's fair to say, were well aware that the enjoyment factor had diminished! Although I wanted out at QPR, I didn't want to quit my job entirely and thankfully they were all pretty understanding about that. There were other things I did want to focus on – for example, expanding the coverage of county cricket and building up to the big DeGale-Groves fight that was finally happening in the summer. Maybe it was also the case that I'd been in the same role for too long – it was more than six years since I'd taken over from Dave Evans, which was more time than I'd spent in total at the *Recorder*. But I hadn't envisaged the QPR connection being something I'd ever want to give up.

As agreed, during the next couple of months I began the process of handing over to George Cooper, who had already covered for me a few times earlier in the season. Coops reported on the games against Hull – when Rangers should have sealed promotion – and Watford, when they finally did. Conditional on the outcome of the FA tribunal, of course – it remained a possibility that the club could have points deducted. On that basis, though, I wanted to at least supervise some kind of souvenir promotion supplement – and the only practical way I could do that was by turning again to the past. I spoke to three players from a previous QPR promotion campaign – Mark Lazarus on 1966-67, Terry Fenwick on 1982-83 and Kevin Gallen on 2003-04. As with the other past player interviews I'd done, it was enormously enjoyable to speak to them, discuss their recollections and put the whole thing together around a centre-page spread on the current season. I was also determined to ensure that the supplement looked visually impressive – which would have been impossible if I'd used the new-look Archant templates.

Until April, each of the London titles had a distinctive appearance, but the company decided on a general redesign to make them all standardised, therefore easier and cheaper to put together. Sensible enough in theory – the flaw in the plan was that the new look was utterly abysmal. The headline fonts were ugly and underwhelming, the page design was rigid and full of 'bits and pieces' such as fact boxes, which we were instructed to make use of at every opportunity, and the colour scheme itself was totally unimaginative. Black and red, that was it – no place for the blue-and-white motif we'd always used for the QPR pages. No way was I prepared to produce a promotion supplement that looked like dross, so I insisted on using the old page design and colour scheme. Even if I say so myself, it looked a whole lot better!

I took some copies of the supplement along to Loftus Road for the final game of the season against Leeds, although at that stage they could still have been rendered redundant. The main reason for attending the game was that I'd continued to do some bits and pieces for BBC London during the course of the season and they'd asked if I was available to help with the commentary for QPR World. No problem with that, although I admit to feeling slightly nauseous by the time kick-off came around. By then, the FA verdict had been delivered – and the club had basically got away with it. Guilty on two charges, the rest not proven and a fine of less than £1m. That meant absolutely nothing to a club who now stood to collect a Premier League windfall. The only genuinely meaningful punishment would have been a points deduction that pushed Rangers into the play-off places – and I'd still have backed the team to go up the hard way. But the FA bottled it, having allowed the entire saga to drag on for not just weeks, but months. For me, it just felt sickening to hear Paul Morrissey read out the FA verdict on the pitch before the game – to the sound of raucous cheers all around the ground. As if breaking the rules and effectively getting away with it were cause for delirious celebration? It emphasised again why I just didn't feel part of this. Time to go.

Once the final whistle went, I just slipped out of the press box, down the stairs and out into South Africa Road. The rest of them could spend all afternoon dancing around with the Championship trophy or whatever they wanted to do. I just wanted to get home. It was four and a half years before I walked down that street again.

# 14

# TONY, JUST STOP MAKING THE SAME OLD MISTAKES

### (February 2013)

It wasn't quite the clean break I'd expected, at least not during the next two years. Having signed off for the season with a parting shot at Briatore and Ecclestone – incredibly, it was Amit and Ishan Saksena who appeared to take the rap for the Faurlin fiasco – I had plenty of other things to occupy my schedule. Middlesex were up and running in their first season back at the top level of county cricket, so I was spending more time at Lord's and increasing the coverage across all titles. There was a good deal to write about the DeGale-Groves fight – in fact, they held the main press event beforehand at Dale Youth Club, the amateur gym on the ground floor of Grenfell Tower where the pair had both trained as teenagers. It still makes me shiver to think about what happened six years later, when the block caught fire and so many people lost their lives. Yet the way in which QPR responded to the tragedy on their doorstep, raising funds for those who had lost their relatives and their homes, was also heart-warming – the sort of thing that would probably never have been considered under the previous regime.

Coops and I both ended up going to watch QPR's pre-season friendly at Harrow Borough – but, whereas his target was to unearth some Rangers copy, I was focussed on the non-league side's preparations for the new campaign. All a bit strange and I can't deny I wasn't mildly embarrassed to be greeted with an effusive hug from Gianni! 'You see, we did it, we're in the Premier League,' he kept saying. The sheer nerve of the man – was he actually claiming credit for Rangers' promotion? Presumably. Still, I smiled back and went along with

Gianni's nonsense one last time while Coops sat there, doing his best not to laugh.

I'd made it clear that, while I was still responsible for the sports section as a whole, it was entirely up to him how he wanted to deal with coverage of QPR. If I could help at all, I'd be happy to – and that included reporting on the odd match here and there, as long as it wasn't at Loftus Road. But I must say it did feel somewhat weird when Rangers kicked off their first Premier League match in 15 years and I found myself a few miles up the road, at Wembley Cricket Club, who were about to make certain of promotion to the next level of the county league. I kept an eye on my phone during the afternoon and, while part of me was shocked to see Rangers getting a pasting from Bolton, I have to admit I was also mildly amused that this embarrassment, after all the crowing and bragging that had gone on, was the way QPR marked their top-flight comeback.

Some people may be wondering why I continued to stay away – by the start of the season, after all, Briatore and Ecclestone were some way down the line in terms of selling up. While that was something I welcomed, of course, I wanted to wait and see what, if anything, might change under the new owner, Tony Fernandes. What transpired was a huge improvement in terms of PR awareness – and the same utter cluelessness when it came to football matters. Of course, fans of any team promoted to the Premier League would expect some targeted recruitment, to try and bridge the gap to the top level. QPR signed virtually an entirely new team in a hurry before the end of the transfer window – and that was the ludicrous policy that became the norm under Fernandes. His good intentions weren't in doubt, his naivety was exposed time and again by a succession of managers and agents. I had no time for it – which isn't to say I didn't hope the team would find their feet and manage to survive in the Premier League. I watched the Chelsea home game on TV with great delight – the Loftus Road crowd created an unwelcoming atmosphere that you could see the majority of the Chelsea players hadn't anticipated and I celebrated the 1-0 victory just as much as any other fan.

However, I was visiting plenty of other football grounds. Archant had set up a website called London24 – the idea being, as the name suggested, that it would cover the capital city as a whole and fill the gaps where the company didn't run a print newspaper. The thinking was, quite reasonably, that marketing a London-wide product made a lot of commercial sense in the build-up to the

2012 Olympic Games. There were also gaps to be filled in terms of other sports – especially football – and I suggested to Matt Diner, who had been appointed to lead the site's sports content, that I might be able to help in that regard. Matt seemed agreeable to the idea – and promptly dispatched me to a 9am press conference at Millwall's training ground near Bromley! Not the easiest assignment during the London rush hour – suddenly I realised I shouldn't have complained about John Gregory's early starts at Harlington – but I was keen to give it a go. During one of my visits to Millwall I was able to get a word with Patrick Agyemang, who had found himself shunted out there on loan and was none too impressed at his treatment by Neil Warnock. The manager had played him in two of QPR's first three games, but then left him out of the 25-man squad without warning after a flood of signings on deadline day.

I also got to cover plenty of games for London24 – at Fulham, Brentford, Charlton, Millwall, Crystal Palace and even AFC Wimbledon and Barnet – and I really enjoyed the challenges it presented. Firstly, of course, I had to focus solely on online content – so it was all about getting the match report written, finding images and uploading both and then looking for quotes-led stories. That meant 'doing my research' as Jim, the man on the radio, used to say – if not actually do – and in some ways it could be more interesting than reporting on one club, where you already knew all the issues and angles of interest.

Going back to Warnock, I felt the manager was on thin ice. He'd been fortunate to escape a disrepute charge after making it crystal clear he couldn't care less about the League Cup, in which Rangers were knocked out by Rochdale, and the 6-0 thrashing at Fulham in October had been an utter shambles. I went to the game at the Emirates on New Year's Eve, along with my Arsenal-supporting cousin – I have quite a few of those, actually! – and, although QPR lost by just the odd goal, the performance was totally uninspiring. In the build-up to the match, I'd done a feature with Bradley Allen, looking back at the 1994 New Year's Eve game against Arsenal, feted by Gunners supporters as 'the one where Jensen scored'. They seem to forget that Bradley, along with Kevin Gallen and Andy Impey, also found the net to earn Rangers a 3-1 victory at Highbury! Coops seemed quite willing to give me free rein as far as those nostalgia features were concerned and I put together similar pieces with Clive Wilson and Peter Hucker, among others.

I also volunteered to cover the FA Cup third-round tie at Milton Keynes Dons a week later which, quite frankly, represented another shocking display by the team. Rangers were lucky to get a 1-1 draw with a last-minute equaliser and personally I was neither surprised nor sorry to see Warnock handed his cards. I know most supporters will disagree, but I believe the decision to sack Warnock was one of the few things Fernandes got absolutely right. He's never kept a team in the top division, either before or since, and that QPR side were going only one way in my opinion.

What the QPR chairman got wrong, however, was that he rushed to appoint the first out of work Premier League manager whose name was brought to his attention. And sadly, despite his mantra of 'lessons learned', Fernandes repeated the same mistake less than a year later, replacing the hapless Mark Hughes with Harry Redknapp – totally the wrong choice for QPR but the first name that was whispered into the chairman's ear. However, I thumbed through my contacts book to find someone who ticked two boxes – knowledge of both Hughes and of QPR – and came up with Paul Jones, the former Wales goalkeeper. I'd got on well with Paul during his time at Loftus Road and he had plenty to say about the incoming manager, making what turned out to be an accurate prediction. 'I'd think Mark will have the opportunity to bring in one or two strikers and he can attract better players because of his own name in the game, the fact he was a top player at the top level.'

Fair enough – you'd probably say Djibril Cisse and Bobby Zamora fell into the category Paul described and ultimately they both did enough, particularly Cisse, to keep Rangers up by the skin of their teeth that season. I went round to watch the final-day game at Manchester City on TV with my old friend Richard – eight years on from our triumphant trip to Hillsborough – and, while it turned into a dramatic finish to the title race, I didn't really feel any tension on behalf of QPR. My feeling for some weeks had been that Rangers' fate would ultimately rest on whether relegation rivals Bolton could muster the points they needed. They didn't, which was a big let-off, but I'd seen enough to conclude Fernandes was far too foolish to do things differently next time.

I had next to no input on the QPR coverage during that summer – aside from a contribution I'd much prefer not to have made. Along with every other Rangers supporter of my era, I felt numb and deeply saddened to learn of Alan McDonald's sudden death from a heart attack while playing golf. Not only was he a player whose courage and commitment to the cause I'd admired for many years, but someone I'd enjoyed getting to know better during his time as assistant manager. I emailed one of the London24 guys and asked if he'd mind uploading a personal tribute to the site – it was something I felt needed to be done and, in all honesty, it needed a QPR fan to write it. I can't recall many occasions when just writing has made me particularly emotional, but this was one of them. I concluded with:

*It's inevitable that, as you grow older, the heroes of your youth begin to die. But I'm sure every QPR fan who watched him commanding the back four for so long will agree: it was far, far too soon to lose Alan McDonald.*

We ran a more detailed tribute to Macca in the next print edition and I spoke to Bradley Allen and Peter Hucker, both of them former team-mates who spoke warmly about how great he'd been to play alongside – and to socialise with off the field too! Hucker summed up how I think most QPR fans felt about Macca, saying, 'Fans appreciate two things – outstanding skill and total commitment. When Macca pulled on the shirt, you knew he'd give it his all.'

Obviously obituary writing – certainly in this context – is something you don't want to be doing very often, but you at least want to feel you've done justice to the deceased. I did another one the following season when former Rangers manager Dave Sexton passed away, and, although I'd never met him personally and been too young to watch his team, the ex-players I spoke to were able to paint a vivid picture of the man he'd been.

Along with my London24 activities, I also spent a certain amount of time reporting on non-league clubs for the paper. Wealdstone, as I've already mentioned, were my favourites and during those couple of seasons they put together a memorable run to the semi-finals of the FA Trophy, as well as losing out twice in the play-offs. The first of those defeats involved an horrendous midweek coach journey to Lowestoft, with two seats occupied by myself and Jon Batham, who reported for the rival Trinity newspaper group. Lowestoft's only in Suffolk, but it's one of those places that takes forever to get to – and I was struck by how hostile an environment it was when we arrived. Let's just say the officials tended to favour the home side – and the local journalists, even allowing for some understandable pro-Lowestoft bias, were about as blinkered as it's possible to be! It was an eye-opener and the interminable journey back wasn't much fun, it must be said. I was reminded of the time I'd flown back from

Newcastle with the West Ham squad – but at least on that occasion we were home in less than an hour.

Hendon were another club who provided me with a couple of interesting days out – they got to play at Luton and then Aldershot in the FA Cup and were actually quite unlucky to lose the second of those ties, 2-1. I was quite proud of my achievement in convincing Junior Lewis, the former Leicester player, to agree to an interview – he'd scored Hendon's winning goal the last time they'd beaten a league side and was now back at the club as a coach. But he made it clear he wasn't all that keen to talk and it took a fair bit of persuasion before he eventually relented.

However, by far the most bizarre story I covered on the non-league beat was the one that involved Wembley. No, not the national stadium – the Combined Counties League club of that name, who played just down the road, five levels below the EFL and in front of double-figure crowds. I took a phone call in the office one day from a lady with an American accent, who explained she was considering a proposed business arrangement with Brian Gumm, the chairman of Wembley FC – and could I vouch for his good character? It was a strange one – I could count the number of conversations I'd ever had with Brian on the fingers of one hand – but he'd always seemed like a decent bloke and I knew he and his wife had basically been running the club for over 20 years. So I basically told my trans-Atlantic caller as much, she thanked me and I thought no more about it until a few months later, when Budweiser got in touch to announce a three-year sponsorship deal with the club! Oh yes, and Terry Venables was on board as Wembley's new technical adviser.

It was incredible stuff, really. Budweiser sponsored the FA Cup at that time and they were keen to make a commitment to grass-roots football as well – so the carrot of a club called Wembley was clearly irresistible. Suddenly Wembley's FA Cup ties would be shown live on social media channels and a host of recently retired international players were available for selection – names such as Martin Keown, Ray Parlour, Graeme Le Saux, Brian McBride and Claudio Caniggia! All quite surreal, as was the notion of attending a formal press conference at Wembley's Vale Farm ground, with BBC presenter Mark Chapman acting as MC before the players were introduced. I can't remember the name of the PR company who arranged the whole thing for Budweiser, but I wanted to burst out laughing when one of them asked me on my way into the ground, 'Are you excited?!' I mean, you may have had fun putting together all those flowery press releases, but I'm afraid it'll take more than that to genuinely melt the stony heart of a cynical hack.

Still, it gave me the opportunity to interview David Seaman – who was also on board with the whole thing, purely to coach Wembley's goalkeepers rather than making a comeback himself though. 'I'm getting on a bit and I don't want any young whipper-snapper running round saying he scored past me!' he said with that distinctive Yorkshire chuckle. As well as discussing Wembley, Seaman was also happy to give his thoughts on recent QPR signing Rob Green – which came in useful for a feature leading up to the 2012-13 season. Of course, I'd naively assumed that a newly arrived international goalkeeper might have joined the club as their first choice. I should have realised that the grand plan at QPR involved signing another international keeper just a few weeks later.

If there was one single transfer that confirmed the club were completely out of control, it was the signing of the vastly overrated Julio Cesar. Utter madness, however they tried to dress it up with nonsense about 'ambition' and 'competition for places'. They also brought in four central-midfield players during that transfer window – why would you ever need so many people for the same position in one go? It might have been more excusable if the club had been recouping any of their outlay through sales, but they weren't – for the most part, players left for free or had their contracts cancelled. Sadly, Rangers fans had got used to this kind of thing throughout the years Gianni had been in charge of buying and selling. It came to appear normal for the club to sign ten or 12 players every transfer window and this was all a continuation of that policy. But the stakes – and sums of money involved – were now far higher than they'd been before.

While QPR's expensively assembled squad floundered at the foot of the Premier League, I kept well out of it, basically. I could have got more involved again a few months into the season when Coops – through no fault of his own, I hasten to add – was made redundant in another round of Archant cost-cutting. But I really wasn't interested, beyond covering one or two away games here and there, which I did – including a pleasant trip down memory lane to Upton Park. For the remainder of that season, the paper's QPR coverage nosedived to minimal, with the London24 staff reporting on matches and supplying reaction stories when required. I was even less inclined to pick up the reins again once it became evident that Fernandes's final throw of the dice was to turn to Redknapp! Rather like recruiting a fox to provide security for your chickens. In a way, it was almost comical to hear Redknapp refer to the chairman 'having his pants pulled down' when you knew that was the exact scenario that would be repeated over and over again. Apart from anything else, Fernandes was far too easily led by Twitter followers, eagerly egging him on to sign more and more players – which made it an obvious recipe for disaster.

Speaking to a number of former QPR players, those who had played for the club under Terry Venables, Jim Smith and Gerry Francis – all managers who led Rangers to top-five finishes – they agreed that one of the reasons it worked had been the make-up of the squad. So many of them had been either players who came through the youth set-up or players who joined QPR from smaller clubs and viewed this as their big chance to make it. Either way, the extra motivation was there for them – they 'wanted it', basically. Contrast that with the likes of Park Ji-sung, Jose Bosingwa and countless others – they were on the way down, not up. Why would any of them feel motivated to perform for QPR? One of the few exceptions at around that time was Clint Hill, who freely admitted it mattered to him because of the career he'd had – after kicking around at Tranmere and Stoke, joining QPR had been his opportunity to make it at the top level.

Another unwelcome hangover from the Briatore regime could be found in the chairman's continuing determination to portray Rangers as something they weren't. While there were fewer references to brands and projects, Fernandes seemed to be obsessed with the notion of moving the club to a 40,000-seater stadium. It was pie in the sky, an absolutely ludicrous idea because there wasn't – and isn't – any way QPR have the fanbase to justify a stadium of that size. Back when my brother and I had season tickets in the Loft – and Rangers were an established mid-table Premier League team – attendances could vary somewhere between 8,000 and 15,000, unless the visitors were Manchester United, Liverpool or one of our London rivals. Those, by and large, were the only games when Loftus Road's capacity of just under 20,000 would be reached. Why, then, might anyone realistically expect a club who weren't able to hold down a Premier League spot for more than one or two seasons to double that crowd? I don't see it as defeatist or negative to say that. QPR aren't a massive club – and that's OK. As Steve Wicks had said, we used to thrive on the chance to punch above our weight, giving a bloody nose to teams who regarded themselves as bigger fish than ourselves.

I could just about accept the theory of hiring Redknapp as a short-term gamble in the hope of staving off relegation – but, once that had failed, Fernandes should have sacked him. It wasn't as if the team went down fighting – on the contrary, their record under Redknapp was relegation form even without the abysmal start they'd had under Hughes. I wrote what turned out to be my final QPR-related contribution to the paper at the end of that season, arguing the case for a manager who could get more out of the players he inherited rather than following the predictable Redknapp solution – sign more of them!

By this time, I was more tempted to have another crack at reporting on one club – but not QPR. My long-standing colleague Paul Chronnell, who had covered Arsenal for around 14 years – although they'd only had one manager in that time! – was off to work for a national paper and so the opportunity was there for someone else to pitch in with the Gunners and work on the *Islington Gazette* and *Ham & High* titles. It appealed to me – Arsenal weren't at the top of the tree any more, but they were still one of the country's highest-profile clubs and Champions League regulars, even if they rarely got anywhere near winning it. So I said farewell to *the Times* that summer, albeit with a certain degree of reluctance. Those eight and a bit years remain my longest stint on any paper and the one that meant most to me.

I suppose I'd hoped the Arsenal post might be a means of recapturing the good times I'd had when I was involved with West Ham, but in all honesty it wasn't. The football I got to watch was great quality – getting to watch the likes of Bayern Munich was a rare treat and I got to cover two FA Cup finals, both of which ended with the Gunners lifting the trophy. Facilities at the Emirates were superb – the whole place had an unmistakeable aura of class about it. But in terms of getting to do any interesting interviews or write any stories that actually felt worthwhile, my Arsenal experience didn't really deliver. While there were some very nice people among the club's media department, their senior people really weren't interested in facilitating different content for the local papers, which was a shame. I remember being left literally open-mouthed by Arsenal's head honcho, Mark Gonella, when he abruptly ushered Arsene Wenger away from a conversation with a group of journalists. Gonella managed to better that on another occasion, when Per Mertesacker was the interviewee – the startled expression on Mertesacker's face was quite a sight as he was basically cut off in full flow.

I did once have the good fortune to get an interview with Hector Bellerin all to myself, then there was also a sit-down chat with Isaac Hayden before he moved on to better things at Newcastle – but those were very much the exception rather than the norm. One aspect of the club that the media department did actively encourage me to cover was Arsenal Ladies, and I was quite happy to do that, partly because it meant walking just around the corner for their home matches at Boreham Wood! On top of that, Arsenal were still one of the leading names in women's football, which meant a fairly regular diet of cup finals and European ties on the menu and it was interesting to speak to players in the very top bracket, such as Steph Houghton, Rachel Yankey and Casey Stoney.

Did it all serve to distract me from events at Loftus Road? Overall it probably did serve that purpose, because 2013-14 was the first season since I'd starting watching QPR that I didn't witness a single fixture. And 2014-15 was the second. Absence, the saying goes, makes the heart grow fonder – but it really didn't in this instance. I'm sure my friends and family – certainly my brother, at least, who didn't think much of the way the club was run but hadn't let it diminish his support – couldn't really understand why I felt so disconnected from it all. Maybe it's partly a character trait, a flaw I suppose, that turns me against things I care about when they take such a drastically wrong turn. My instinctive reaction is to say it's better for them to fail – they need to be taught a lesson to put them back on the right track. Without sinking too deep into a political commentary, it's not too unlike the way my feelings towards the Labour Party developed around the same time. I was a firm believer in New Labour, I voted for Tony Blair and Gordon Brown as well. But once Ed Miliband began to disown their legacy and also initiated the catastrophic changes that enabled the party to slip into the clutches of the hard left, it was vital – in my view – for Labour to be overwhelmingly rejected, humiliated at the ballot box. If that meant voting Conservative, to force Labour to change their ways, I saw it as a price worth paying.

I appreciate many will disagree, which is fine – and I also appreciate many will be unable to comprehend how I can honestly say I wanted Derby to beat QPR in the 2014 Championship play-off final. I was asked if I wanted to go to the match and declined. In fact, I didn't even watch it on TV. There was no way I could see myself going to Wembley, trying to show my pride in QPR – because I was ashamed of the club. The players – with the exception of one or two like Clint Hill – were no more than a bunch of short-term mercenaries, assembled on the basis that if you stockpile enough of them sooner or later you'll stumble on a winning formula. If Rangers were promoted, I knew that would mean the following season would be an utter waste of time – with Redknapp handed yet more funds to fritter away on has-beens and immediate relegation, with the club in even worse shape financially. Defeat at Wembley might have meant Redknapp's departure that summer and a chance for the club to get back on track. When teams reach a Wembley final, you expect a number of fair-weather fans to come streaming out the woodwork. I retreated deeper into the woodwork, you could say.

The way it turned out, with Bobby Zamora's last-minute winner sending Rangers back to the Premier League, I know I made the right decision to swerve the game. To coin that phrase of David McIntyre's, I would have been the only one sober at the party!

Next season came and went and, just as I'd envisaged, it was basically a wasted year before the club gradually began to change direction, out of financial necessity rather than any kind of moral revelation. But what I was hearing from people including Sean Gallagher, who had recently taken over my old job on *the Times*, seemed encouraging – and, surprising myself, I agreed to join Richard and his son, as well as my brother, to watch Rangers play Preston at Loftus Road. No particular reason, other than the same reason anybody chooses to go and see a football match – I thought I might enjoy it. Richard told me later he'd feared I would pull out at the last minute – because Warnock was back, taking over as caretaker after Redknapp's successor, Chris Ramsey, had stepped down. Maybe a couple of years earlier he'd have been right and I'd have thrown a wobbly, recalling how problematic Warnock had been to deal with. But for whatever reason, I wasn't all that bothered – just don't expect me to join in with the chants of 'Neil Warnock's blue and white army', I stressed!

Going back to Loftus Road after four and a half years was something akin to a return visit to your old school. Most of the sights, sounds and smells remain completely familiar, although naturally you also notice the changes that have taken place. We sat in the Loft Upper Stand and it felt good to be back there, in the place I'd sat and cheered, sung and celebrated, got irate at players and referees alike. The game itself wasn't that memorable – it finished 0-0, which seemed appropriate enough. My first game at Loftus Road had also been a scoreless draw, against Watford, so maybe my second 'first game' was destined to finish the same way.

That experience didn't spark an immediate desire to start watching every single QPR match again, but I knew I could now go back to Loftus Road and enjoy it again and did exactly that a couple more times during the next year. I suppose you'd say that was one psychological hurdle overcome, but there was one more that still remained on my to-do list – covering a game at Loftus Road from the press box again.

# FULL-TIME

Whatever other accusations might be hurled in my direction, I don't think anyone could say I only turn up for the glamour. Wigan Athletic, on a Tuesday evening in February 2017 – that was the fare on offer when I returned to the Loftus Road press box, for the first time in over six years. However, I genuinely enjoyed watching the game, I enjoyed the fact that Rangers won it 2-1, and I enjoyed the whole experience. Which was just as well – I probably needed a shot in the arm because at that moment I was fairly short on journalistic options.

I'd left Archant a fortnight earlier, along with my two remaining sports desk colleagues, Ben Pearce and Sean Gallagher. Our departures had been in the pipeline for several months – the new people who were calling the shots had made it resoundingly clear we weren't their cup of tea. And they weren't mine either – unless I liked my tea stone cold, with a taste like dishwater and a steady growth of mould on top. I think we all knew it was a case of either walking out or waiting to be paid to go – and in the end it was the latter. We discussed the whole thing at length, tried to help each other out in terms of advice and basically stuck together, which I certainly appreciated and hopefully the other two lads did as well. While I was sad to see the team breaking up, I'm pleased it seems to have worked out well for all of us in the long run.

At the time, however, I didn't have a plan in terms of what I was going to do next. But David McIntyre had been nagging me for a while to consider going back to QPR – and I was keen to contribute to the West London Sport website he ran. With traditional local newspapers all cutting back – and, it has to be said, basically dumbing down their sports coverage, it was even more important to have an outlet that would do the job properly and offer some quality journalism. Somehow I was nervous about returning after so long, yet David kept assuring me nobody in the QPR media department or anywhere else would have a problem with it. 'OK, you've convinced me,' I said. 'I'll see you there on Tuesday.'

He was absolutely right. Again, it felt a little bit like a school reunion! I had a good chat with Ian Taylor and Paul Morrissey, caught up with people like Tony Incenzo and Brian Melzack, who I hadn't seen for a while, and really noticed a marked contrast in the whole atmosphere around the press area. There had always been a steady undercurrent of tension during the Briatore era, but now it all seemed more relaxed – and Ian and Paul certainly did too, more like they had been in the early days. You might say it was weird, purely because it wasn't weird.

Slowly, I got back into the groove, doing some match reports, some player interviews – and even QPR player ratings, something I'd always been sceptical about! The great thing about player ratings, as I've learned, is that they usually provoke debate and argument. Someone watching the match from a different part of the ground will always have a different view of who performed well and who didn't, and they're not slow to let you know what they think of your assessment! I also learned how useful it can be to be part of an operation that's online only, because the space you have to play with is unlimited. So whether you don't have very much material, or content coming out of your ears, it doesn't matter. Sometimes player interviews will be on offer, sometimes they won't – and I don't get stressed about that now. It doesn't have a big impact in the way it did when I had a certain number of column inches to fill every week – and hopefully that increases my enjoyment of matchdays as well.

Which is, I suppose, the bottom line. Soon I found myself punching the air again when the ball hit the back of the opposition net, feeling enthused by a good Rangers performance and disgruntled if the team had failed to turn up. I got to know people around the club again and looked forward to seeing familiar faces. My freelance work elsewhere limits the number of games I can get to, but that's fine – most supporters have to be selective for one reason or another. The important thing is that, once again, Loftus Road has become a place where I do feel at home.

Most football fans will vehemently insist that support for your club is always unconditional. I used to believe that too. But the nature of the relationship is one-sided – the club, to state the obvious, can never love you back. It may become dramatically changed from the entity you originally attached yourself to. Then, as in any relationship, you may have to agonise as to whether you stay or go. In this case, however, even if you walk, the door's never entirely closed.

These days, I feel Rangers are in a far better place, albeit that financial necessity has forced them back to doing what they neglected for so many years

– trying to develop players and sell them on rather than buying them ready-made. I have confidence in the people who, at the time of writing, are doing their best to achieve that and I hope I'll be around to see the club punching above their weight again in the future.

Looking back over my own experiences and trying to articulate them has been, for want of a better word, cathartic. I'll always be thankful that I had the opportunity to report on QPR for so many years and I think I've gained a better understanding of why I felt as I did during and after that period. It's also reminded me that, at least for a time, there surely wasn't a better job in the world.

Printed in Great Britain
by Amazon

53836339R00111